A
Sentient
Perspective

A guided tour to attaining our sanity

By Whickwithy

D1343711

The Sentient Perspective

All rights reserved

Published by Whickwithy

whickwithy@gmail.com

Cover art: NASA/JPL-Caltech/T. Megeath (Harvard-Smithsonian CfA)

ISBN: 978-0-9971412-3-8

The Sentient Perspective by Whickwithy

Printed by Ingram-Sparks/KDP

Available where books are sold

First published 2019

Also worth reading by Whickwithy
Sentience, 2019 revision
ISBN: 978-0-997-1412-0-7

A missive for mankind

Discourse on sentience, sanity, reason, and emotional stability

"Know thyself"
- The Oracle of Delphi

"Wisdom begins in wonder"
"The unexamined life is not worth living"
"Let him that would move the world first move himself"
"The greatest way to live is to be what we pretend to be"
"From the deepest desires often come the deadliest hate"
- Socrates

"Once, while Thales was gazing upwards while doing astronomy, he fell into a well. A Thracian serving-girl made fun of him, since he was eager to know the things in the heavens but failed to notice that which was right in front of him."
- Plato
~Thales is often noted as the originator of philosophy

"Darkness cannot drive out darkness; only light can do that.
Hate cannot drive out hate; only love can do that."
- Martin Luther King, Jr.

"The smell of a world that is burned"
- Jimi Hendrix

Contents

Whickwithy

A Sentient Perspective

The Japanese have a saying, "One who asks a question feels like a fool for a moment. One who refuses to ask a question is a fool for a lifetime." Humanity has avoided asking a few all-important questions for all the long millennia of its existence.

Ironically, those questions we have refused to ask can fulfill our existence. We have remained with one foot in the realm of the beast and only one in the realm of the human sentient experience without answering those crucial unasked questions.

If, surprisingly, you think in terms of mankind being inherently sane, rational, emotionally stable, good, and possessing an ability to care that is forged in steel, you will not be disappointed. If you think that the brutality and the misery of mankind are inherent or that mankind is only an advanced monkey needing more taming and training, you have a surprise in store. There is more to mankind that you think. Self-awareness changed us more than we admit.

It is often said that perceptions are reality. Not exactly. More to the point, perceptions are the interpretations of existence, whether valid or not. Being fully self-aware changed reality radically. As long as we continue to interpret a faulty and, thereby perceive a delusional version of reality, we will remain befuddled and defeated. Perceptions must match this unique reality of self-awareness in order to fulfill the human experience.

We can gain our humanity by unlocking the human perspective. We are not the witless automatons we pretend to be. Shunning the all-important questions has incited a bizarre conflict causing confusion and delusion within the human experience.

Imagine a world in which humanity cares for itself. *That* is what a fully sentient race would do. A race that has gained emotional balance, honor, integrity, and reason cares for itself.

Humanity is a breathtaking work of art that refuses to accept its own astonishing existence. Realizing a single, most important aspect of our heightened sentience of uncompromising self-awareness unleashes mankind's grace and wonder.

In one disastrous way we continue to mimic the beast. We only become fully human by removing this last remnant of the beast that defeats a self-aware, sentient, human existence.

Perceptions

A race's awareness isn't like a light bulb turning on. It is the slow, increasingly comprehensive perception of existence and self. Delusions and confusion derail those perceptions when nonsense is substituted for insights, bombast for reason. Humanity's exceptional sentient state of self-awareness is nurtured by a prodigious brain, hyperawareness, and curiosity. It is compromised by nonsense.

In the distant past, mankind created stories to explain existence in order to comfort mankind's desire for comprehension, regardless of whether the stories made sense or not. Our ancient ancestors led themselves into many erroneous conclusions with these stories and, at least, one significant disaster in understanding that still remains.

Some of those early explanations were incredibly creative, intriguing, and completely wrong. They were just the most pleasing or obvious extrapolations that our undeveloped intellect could agree upon without further knowledge and wit. As an example, the Sun and the universe do not revolve around the Earth but that thought satisfied for a very long time.

It is not surprising that certain aspects of existence were misinterpreted. The newly emerging hyperawareness was assaulted by an enormous amount of input. We felt an urgent need to explain what baffled us. The information required in order to form a sound decision, though, was not always available.

Once consensus is achieved on some matter by some group, overturning any misinterpretations becomes exceedingly difficult. Humanity's attachment to faulty insights seems curiously extreme. For instance, those who first dared suggest such relatively unimportant prospects as that the Earth might spin on its axis were enthusiastically persecuted.

We are not stupid. We are, though, inhibited by past errors as long as they remain unchallenged. One such error concerning our self-aware perspective has thoroughly duped our existence. We have continued to build on this particular delusion to remain a beast.

The critically flawed insight resides uncomfortably close to our identity. It concerns our own self-aware existence. It has created a blind spot that is overwhelmingly accepted, embellished, and reinforced. The delusion increasingly disconcerts mankind's perspective as the inconsistencies become blatantly obvious to our ever-heightening awareness and perceptions of reality.

An overpowering desire to avoid its close inspection has allowed the misinterpretation to remain. We have not relished the implied answer. How wrong we have been. The *actual* answer is truly breathtaking. We are far more than we imagine.

There has been something horribly wrong from the beginning. We have accepted a creative fabrication that is utterly misleading. The situation is superficially intimidating and disturbs the mindless context of the beast. Its simple, elegant resolution is something only a human could even begin to comprehend.

Significant self-improvement is not within the means of a witless animal. It requires a developed sentient perspective to comprehend a situation and advanced intellect to change it.

This particular misperception is so disturbing that it creates inconsistencies that conflict with our reasoning. As such, it has substantially affected the development of our reason, emotional balance, and very existence. The more we understand about this universe and ourselves, the more it disturbs.

This shortcoming in our perceptions of existence, due to our animal heritage, remains troubling to our self-awareness. Its subtle, complex nuances confounded and disturbed our ancient ancestors' simple understandings. The terribly convoluted, conflicted perspective that resulted has carried forward unabated.

The subject that we have so thoroughly avoided caused us to bury our heads in the sand. A gaping hole exists in our self-awareness wreaking awful results. The *seeming* truth has been too painful to face. The *real* truth is nothing short of awe-inspiring and extraordinary. The simple and gratifying answer to this puzzling predicament is profoundly important. It unleashes our humanity, and ends our mimicry of the beast.

Self-awareness, long ago, provided an puzzling insight. We have bludgeoned our way around its realization like a beast, thus avoiding a sentient perspective. Our expanding consciousness can now acknowledge the puzzling situation for what it is and our burgeoning intellect can resolve the puzzle. Something more is required of us.

Our aversion to and the baffling aspects of the puzzle are reflected in our earliest myths.

Myths

A myth is a story that attempts to address some puzzling aspect of reality without the restriction of matching reality in any way. Today, we just call such stories speculative fiction or fantasy.

One elusive aspect of an animal's existence is troubling to our heightened awareness. In our most distant past, it distressed and baffled our newly emerging wit. Certain myths ineptly attempted to highlight the situation, but brought little clarity while misleading to a great extent. Some misled entirely. Increasingly, we just looked away and avoided the puzzle completely.

The puzzle remains extremely obscure as the early bewilderment and inappropriate conclusions remain. The myths vaguely suggest only that there is a crucial quandary. The perplexing vagueness of the myths is a piece of the puzzle.

The myths do little but obscure the situation due to their ambiguity but, also, reveal volumes once the situation is finally understood. Once the true situation and its implications are accepted, one can read between the lines of the myths.

The applicable myths emphasize the confusion surrounding our emergence into self-awareness. They mislead concerning a crucial difference between animals and humans. By continuing to avoid that difference, our perceptions of reality remain distorted. Our existence is tied to, but not dictated by, our animal ancestry. Sentient self-awareness entails much more than being just a smart animal.

Mankind's exceptional intelligence, insightfulness, and self-awareness are differences that begin to distinguish us from all other animals. Due to this, we can perceive and create changes that a common animal cannot even begin to comprehend .... or we can continue to comfort ourselves in delusion. One pivotal delusion concerning the beast remains that utterly destroys a sentient, self-aware perspective.

Identifying and acknowledging this crucial aspect of an animal's existence is essential to attaining the unobstructed perceptions that lead to a sentient perspective. It is something that we can change, but our earliest ancestors considered it just as cast in stone as the cosmos. We must break the delusion in order to empower a key aspect of being human.

Pandora's Box

The myth of Pandora's Box is a remarkable assessment of the dilemma that we still face. It portrays well the confusion as we first began to explore our sentient self-awareness in words. The essence of the myth, once the hyperbole, misogyny, and theodicy of the myth are removed, vaguely reveals the situation.

The essential story is of a box containing a gift for humanity that created chaos in the absence of the hope. This beautifully describes the situation. Its vagueness is understandable due to the authors' limited tools and insights with which to articulate the baffling situation. They could barely express the suspicion that something was wrong. It takes courage and our more sophisticated perspective to elucidate.

The myth has been deemed a description of the seemingly unavoidable dystopian aspects of self-awareness. It is, instead, a remarkable description of the most compelling dilemma that mankind has ever faced and its potential for resolution. Self-awareness did not create the chaos. It only recognized the dilemma that causes chaos. We discount the hope remaining in the box as a preposterous dream. That abandoned hope is, in fact, the only possible way for humanity to leave the beast behind.

One description of Pandora's Box is "a valuable gift that *became* a pandemonium-causing curse in the absence of hope". As you will see, that is a fabulously accurate description.

The myth's reference to hope suggests that mankind could eventually change what seems a curse back into the valuable gift it initially represented. The insight astoundingly and accurately suggests that the chaos of our troubled existence is *not* inherent. We can attain far more than a beastly existence.

Pandora's Box suggests that we could eventually (around three thousand years later, as it turns out) discern the source of hope and finally become wholly human. Accurate, unhindered perceptions of our self-aware reality releases the insight that our intellect can then overcome to defeat the chaos.

The well developed state of our sentience is necessary to fully comprehend what the myth suggests. We can be far more than just smart animals. The brutish approach we have endured for millennia that obscures the situation has been matched by an increasing awareness of the situation.

The myth's most revealing description is that "the divine gift of a jar (box) was opened by a *curious* male". Curiosity is an essential ingredient of our hyperawareness that cannot be avoided. *Accurate* insights into questions raised by curiosity fulfill our sentience. Furtive, delusional excuses to critical questions compromise our sentient perspective, thus releasing chaos. By finally discerning the puzzling source of our delusions, we release the hope of the myth and open the path to become fully human.

The ancient confusion occurred because our wit did not yet match our awareness. The original author(s) of Pandora's Box realized that the puzzle was beyond their current generations' ability to fully grasp and resolve the issue, yet added the intuitive leap that hope remained for later generations to do so. That is nothing short of a remarkably honest, insightful assessment. As we first emerged from our bemused animal state, this myth faced the beast squarely without despair. Embellishments corrupted the myth relegating that hope to a distant dream.

The less scrupulous embellishments of the myth, such as Hesiod's, misled us further into chaos. The application of creativity, a penchant for hyperbole, and the childish desire for a scapegoat resulted in blaming women and distracting us from the actual situation as we began our journey into deceit.

Our earliest awareness was little more than that of an animal. The embellished, simpleton explanations aggravated the discord and chaos, increasing the delusion. We must first honestly articulate the inconsistency that wreaks havoc on our self-awareness. Then, our intellect can easily overcome the anomaly. Hope is released as we perceive the answer to riddle. Mankind becomes whole as we resolve it.

As you begin to understand the real situation that our ancient ancestors faced, you will see that the essence of this myth is courageously honest and amazingly on target. The churlish, vituperative embellishments resulted in thoroughly obscuring the situation, delaying its resolution and our humanity by millennia.

As described in the myth, self-awareness (the box) noted a perplexing situation. The unresolved situation of the gift upends our existence into chaos and discord. We can finally attain the full potential of a human sentient perspective and our formidable intelligence in short order. It is not the slow progress of a beast. Within a single generation, we can begin this magnificent change.

The Garden of Eden

The Garden of Eden is a disastrous embellishment of Pandora's Box. It portrays knowledge, as well as women, as cursed. It implies that we learned something we should not have. In actuality, we have not yet learned enough. This myth dismayingly dismisses sentience as an irredeemable curse. The hopelessness that implies is disturbing and defeating.

The myth longs for the bliss of witless non-sentience, an existence without realizations or shame. That supposed shame is undeserved, except for the fact that we remain only a smart animal blinded to its full potential.

The blinding misrepresentation is that sentience *caused* the problem rather than just highlighting a problem that long preceded our sentient existence. The erroneous logic that animals don't think therefore they are content is horribly wrong. This set us on a path to hopelessly despise our sentient existence and, therefore, ourselves.

'We think, therefore, we are not content' is the worst logic ever stated. It blinds us to the fact that we can overcome the necessary hurdle and, thereby, merit our sentient state. The myth encourages a desire to shed our sentience which is impossible, not to mention insane and absurd. It is surrender to the beast. Ignorance is celebrated.

The myth rues the loss of our animalistic mindlessness. Anything more than an animal's existence is portrayed as a curse. This describes well the genesis and acceptance of our self-induced misery. An honest view provides an end to that misery.

Sentience made us aware of an inconsistency in an animal's existence, nothing more. Animals haven't the wit to identify, much less overcome, that lack. It can only be identified by self-awareness and overcome by intellect. We remain in an unflinching animal's stupor while our hyperawareness notes and, increasingly, emphasizes this missing element that releases us.

The story of the Garden of Eden portrays our very existence as corrupted and cursed. The myth says that, once upon a time, there were two humans that somehow came to exist in a garden of life where they frolicked in joy and witlessness with all of the other animals and everything was copacetic. Right.

Then a woman ruined everything by giving into the temptation of learning something. Right.

What was that temptation? A vague reference is made to some knowledge that ruined everything. The misdirect that it was a woman tempted and a snake that did the tempting would be hilarious if millennia of misery and evasion were not the result.

An unobstructed sentient perspective, which we have not yet attained, is something to admire, not disdain. The beauty of this natural progression is that, once achieved, it transforms our existence. It opens new worlds to perception and clarification.

We cannot fully attain our sentience until we recognize the sham that our ancestors foisted on us and we have endured and embellished ever since. We must finally perceive the situation through the honest lens of a sentient perspective. Our insights, liberated of delusion, open vast uncharted territories. Anything less than a clear sentient perspective leaves us in a bestial stupor filled with confusion, failure, and vulnerable to self-serving deceit.

The perplexing riddle of our existence was first pondered in these myths dating back almost three thousand years. The unresolved riddle has left us baffled and undone. The trap in which we have spent millennia is enshrined in the vagaries of Pandora's Box and reinforced by the callow misinterpretations of reality that embellish both myths and reflects our delusional state.

We have yet to appreciate and accept the most delightful consequence of our emergence beyond the status quo of the feeble-minded animals that preceded us. Mankind, a hyperaware race, only ever needed to study the situation to gain an unobstructed sentient perspective and fulfillment. We need not endure the dystopia caused by remaining suspended somewhere between an animal and sentient state.

Celebration of the 'animal spirit', the human parody of an animal's existence, is enacted in an animal's stupor. It underlines our sentient failure. We are not just an animal with a big brain.

There is something remaining in us that runs counter to our sentience, intelligence, self-awareness, and grace. So far, we are little changed from the cowering beast that crawled out of its cave. Something is still bringing out the beast in mankind. The source of our delusions and its resolution surprise the deluded beast in us while not surprising at all the sentient, self-aware human being that is in everyone of us.

Clarity

Something severely disturbed our earliest ancestors' emerging self-awareness. Unfortunately, rather than face the disturbance, they looked away and blamed awareness itself.

Our self-awareness can never be banished. Attempting to do so only cripples us into chaos. So far, our self-awareness has been duped by delusions. We can accept and easily overcome that which deludes our sentient perspective.

Maybe the most informative description of Pandora's Box is that a curious male released chaos by opening the box and then promptly closed it on the hope that remains within. This describes well the unresolved discrepancy in our midst that was lost in the hubbub of our emergence into sentient self-awareness.

We require clarity to create stability for our formidable capabilities, not delusions. We remain deluded concerning sex. Mankind was provided with the unusual capacity to indulge in the act of sex eye to eye. This emphasizes the element that, when missing, leaves us as no more than a beast. Alongside our formidable capabilities, the troublesome, mindless, selfish context of bestial sex sets in motion an insidious situation. Sex is more than it seems. Its sentient fulfillment makes us human.

This transformative thought is difficult to confront and disastrous to ignore. Early man's brutality and dimwittedness disguised the situation that modern man still unnecessarily endures. It also, inadvertently, hid the simple resolution for millennia. That brutal uncertainty of our ancient ancestors grew from the beast's confusion into full blown sexism, misogyny, delusion, aggravation, frustration, and paranoia which have been all that has distinguished us from our animal predecessors, so far.

Mutually satisfying sex makes us humans. The ability to make love is a *human* endeavor. So far, we have mostly been incapable of achieving that goal. It is *not* a terminal condition. It is a beast's rendition that human insight can easily overcome.

Making love creates stability, fulfills our sentient perspective, releases hope, and ends the chaos. Rutting like an animal is a selfish, self-gratifying bestial act that reduces us. We transcend the beast by achieving the fulfillment of the human, sentient, self-aware mutually satisfying enactment of sex eye to eye. We remain only an animal when sex is performed for the male's gratification only. Resolution has only been delayed by our fearful, duped, ancient avoidance of the subject entirely.

The book, *Sentience*, describes the simple insights required for a man to last as long as he desires. This is the crucial step that enables the complete self-aware, disciplined fulfillment of the human expression of making love eye to eye. The finer points of love-making, which are also discussed and elucidated, are naturally explored once a man is freed from the crippling effect of the failure to last. Finding any way in which to satisfy the woman is a vast improvement beyond the beast. The unassisted eye to eye engagement of mutual satisfaction is the ultimate sentient expression that completely frees us from delusion.

We were not thrown out of paradise. We were offered entry into paradise which we have, so far, rejected. The sexual situation has been faulty since long before sentience emerged. Sentient self-awareness only made the flaw apparent, necessitating its resolution.

Eye to eye sexual engagement continuously hints that there is more to the act of sex than rutting. We became aware that sex contained the prospect of far more than just making babies and women providing for men's satisfaction. Clarity is achieved by admitting the fact. A man not only can, but must, fulfill the sexual experience. Self-awareness leaves no other route to sanity. Insights of intellect easily overcome the dilemma.

The fact that something was lacking became clear to the curious male. Rutting is not enough for a self-aware being. Long ago, the belief became accepted that men could not improve the situation leaving men in utter despair and confusion. Misogyny, sexism and many other demeaning traits are the result.

Animals are driven to procreate. Due to the simple nature of the common animal, their instructions for sex are explicit and iron-clad: reproduce. Survival is at stake and a common animal hasn't the wit to interpret the situation. Due to the dimwitted, obdurate nature of our earliest ancestors, closer to the animal than the human, sentient realization that there is more to sex and resolution through intellect has been delayed by millennia.

The intimidating realization that the female can also achieve complete sexual satisfaction baffled and debilitated early man and they ran for cover. The unreasonable fear of failure shunted it all into obscurity, delaying its final unassisted resolution.

Our intellect continues to wreak havoc in the absence of the emotional stability provided by mutually satisfying sex. Its counterbalancing force is required to fully stabilize a highly intelligent, sentient, self-aware existence.

The caring, human perspective is destroyed in the mindless thrusting of bestial sex. Self-confidence and the finer points of making love are the natural derivatives of a man's success at satisfying his woman. An honorable sentient perspective is as natural as lying eye to eye in the loving tangle that invokes the human imperative for caring.

History lesson

The resultant nonsense, due to the lack of realization and resolution of the sexual quandary, has held center stage for millennia. We have bewilderingly avoided contemplating the ever-present realization, though we cannot help but remain uncomfortably aware. There is no doubt that a lot of men fail to provide sexual satisfaction, the evidence is overwhelming. There is no doubt that we have desperately and foolishly attempted to hide from the dilemma. It is only an animal's lack due to instinct.

So, why did it happen? How did it all begin? This confounding aspect of sex caused rampant confusion as we learned to articulate. We knew something was wrong but, without resolution, had no desire to confront it. We prevaricated and accepted the beast - for millennia.

Once again, Pandora's Box is an excellent starting place. The essence of the story is that mankind was gifted with the wonder of self-awareness (the box) and the potential for loving sex (the gift). Chaos, discord, and rationalizations flourished as our ancestors limited insights failed to resolve the dilemma. Hope waned as we became convinced of the certainty of failure.

Mankind became aware that there should be more to sex than just the man's physical pleasure. Curiosity and self-awareness detected the problem without resolution. The simple context of their existence was unable to overcome the obstacle due to the limited development of their slowly emerging intellect. The question became increasingly uncomfortable. Creativity detached the situation from reality, thus obscuring and locking the lid on the hope that still remained. In desperation, women were blamed rather than men's inability to complete the sentient sexual act that our self-awareness demands.

Sex was wonderful but something was missing. The seemingly unattainable potential drove early man crazy. Newly minted creativity was used to suppress the conscious thought that befuddled and discomfited their dim intellect. It subconsciously became deemed as just as unchangeable as the spinning sky.

If we had been content to only highlight the riddle, all would have proceeded well. But, we slowly gained an increasing desire to make it all go away.

Almost three thousand years ago, some interpretations of Pandora's Box, such as Hesiod's embellishments (the first known *written* version), describe well the offensive, misogynistic, deluding vitriol that emerged to blame women for the chaos. Hesiod's tale is one of the earliest instances of the full blown misogyny that was created in order to hide men's confusion concerning sex. The beast was released and a clear sentient perspective was vanquished, never to see the light of day, until now. Women became absurdly accepted as a curse laid on man. Where is the sentient thought in that preposterous notion?!??!

That first insane interpretation was embraced, providing thorough evidence of just how pervasive the problem has always been. No man (or not enough) stood up and said, "What a crock! Women are the best. Duh! They are the gift! You only need to keep it up!" Instead, "Can't live with them and can't live without them" became the byword. The majority of men desired an excuse to salve their ego in absence of resolution. The last three thousand years have been utterly preposterous and absurd.

The delusions progressed quickly. The Garden Of Eden expanded the curse from just women to encompass thinking (about it especially, but also, in general) and sentience. Reason and thinking were overcome. The self-flogging began. Insanity proliferated into every aspect of our existence creating a bestial dystopia out of the potentially beautiful sentient experience.

The man who beats his wife whether it be verbally or physically, or disparages women, or considers sex his right to be wrangled out of a woman whether or not the woman offers or desires it, is nothing more than an animal that has learned to talk and walk on two legs. The man that retains the slightest shred of misogyny, which is most men, is just a deluded, unenlightened animal.   Where is the human?   The human emerges as a man learns to make love.

What makes this so colossally sad and ironic is that every man *wants* to satisfy his lover.   The unnecessary inability eventually undermines every thought.   Every man *can* fully satisfy their lover with just a little knowledge and no other assistance!

While it would be easy to portray men as the villain, the culprit, that would be a mistake. It would be better to describe the male gender as the bearer of an incomprehensible burden that has baffled men and the human race into oblivion, so far.

Can you imagine the bewilderment early men faced? The idea that animal sex was incomplete was far too much to absorb. Even if this radical concept could have been accepted, there was zero guidance and insight for their simple intellect to overcome the deficiency.   Instincts and the overwhelming desire for sex overrode their wit.   The animal's rutting continued and was justified, forcing mankind to remain nothing more than a beast.

The farce in our existence

Why don't men unabashedly celebrate women?   Men's brutal treatment of women is completely at odds with men's deep desire for sex and also erodes our humanity.   The desire would best be served by making sex appealing to a woman, but...

The reason for our disruption becomes obvious.

The bestial brute treatment of women only coerces, subjugates, disillusions, and/or repels women. It does not lead to a woman's loving interest in sex. The whole farce of our existence is filled with the despicable tactics used to dominate, subjugate, and delude women into engaging in inept sex. It resulted in the domination of every aspect of a woman's life which they have gently fought to overcome for millennia.   A fulfilled loving relationship is not even a remote possibility under such conditions.

The millennia-long brutal mistreatment of women has caused a form of Stockholm Syndrome and prisoner/prison guard mentality that substitutes for an intimate, loving relationship and distorts our whole existence. It instigates the disastrous authority complex.   We become a distorted and deceived beast in the depths of sentient self-aware confusion.

The worst farce of all is the colossal hoax we have played on ourselves from the beginning.   We have maintained the delusion that men are good at sex. Guess who wrote *that* script? Look at the statistics sometime. An *optimistic* estimate is that seventy percent of men are bad at sex. That is far worse than any plague. Considering that the failure is based on subtle instincts inherited from our animal predecessors, it is a problem that all men must overcome. Because of the subtlety of the problem, it is understandable that most men fail. It is easily overcome.

Women will never completely overcome sexism and misogyny until its source, the farcical, failed, loving sexual experience is overcome. Mankind will never experience the grand scheme of a loving sentient existence until the physical embodiment of love becomes acknowledged and common.

The false bravado, pompous acts and rationalizations attributed to manliness are nothing more than a deceit at the very heart of our existence meant to disguise the failure that men despairingly endure that disrupts every aspect of our existence.

The hoax leaves us with a corrupted, deceitful, and dispirited perspective. As self-respect, honesty, and integrity are breached, the kingdom of sentience is surrendered to the beast.

Once men's true sentient nature is fulfilled, the results will be just as spectacular as should be expected.

Another story from our distant past emerged to explain the power of man and woman unleashed. Yin and Yang portrays the forces of man and woman as contrary. They can finally become what they were destined to be. Interconnected forces that are complementary and complete. The forces of Yin and Yang can finally begin to merge into the magnificent work of art that mankind's sentient self-aware perspective represents.

Living with honour

The most commonly accepted belief is that ignorance and, thus, lack of education are what limit mankind. Knowledge is, of course, important, but on its own, has little to do with honour, integrity, and all of the finer, natural qualities of being human. Self-respect, the most fundamental enabling quality, is undermined by the inability to fulfill the sentient sexual imperative: make love, not lust. It is only a small area of knowledge needed to sustain and reinforce the naturally occurring self-respect.

It is not ignorance that produces sexism, misogyny, and sexual offenses. No higher education is required to know these are offensive, worse than bestial. These misbegotten mindsets are rampant throughout all levels of society and learning. Yet, we have avoided facing the source of these egregious behaviours that create our worst issues.

Attempting to overcome these mindsets without overcoming their cause is a delusion and disaster. The futile attempts to train out or punish bad behaviour encapsulates everything we are doing wrong. The beast that is trained or cowed into good behaviour through systems of education or punishment remains a beast. Where is the human? We are more than an untrained monkey. The human is only released by attaining unobstructed self-awareness.

It is not ignorance that induces a man to beat his wife. It is a darkness. Domestic violence and abuse are only one example of the darkness we endure. There is a deceit and frustration that darkens the consciousness at every level. Domestic violence, sexism, misogyny, and sexual offenses exist throughout all walks of life, *all strata of society*, and *all levels of learning*. That is only the beginning of the corruption it causes to our existence.

It is not ignorance that induces mankind's bestial behaviour. We know the problem. We have just conditioned ourselves to ignore it. Bestial sex compromises self-respect in a sentient being, ensures selfish behaviour, and initiates the brute into self-deceit. We have deceived ourselves since the beginning.

Honor and integrity are not missing due to lack of education. They are not acquired accessories. Even the simplest existence can be lived honorably. It all hinges on the retention of self-respect. It is thoroughly vanquished by accepting lust in the absence of the fulfilled sexual experience. Honor and integrity, etc are outgrowths of intact self-respect. Self-respect is the cornerstone to our existence that is compromised by the beast.

In the absence of bringing sex to a human conclusion, our ancient, knuckle-dragging ancestors that were much closer to our animal predecessors lost any chance at retaining self-respect. In absence of resolution, they developed excuses that have become conditioned into the very fabric of our lives distorting every aspect.

The conditioning that developed, in the form of confusing myths and habits of thought, has held us in thrall ever since. Inept sex is not genetic. It is just dumb animal instinct that is repeated by every generation due to the conditioning to accept failure.

Humanity's self-awareness and creativity preceded the wit and insights necessary to overcome bestial sex. Early man was flummoxed. We stupefied ourselves long ago to avoid close inspection of the situation in the absence of an answer. Self-respect was thus abdicated for millennia. We hide in delusions.

The conditioning (brainwashing) to avoid any thought concerning the pertinent sexual situation becomes more elaborate with each generation. Our delusions becomes more complex as our awareness becomes more comprehensive.

Every man would love to make passionate love rather than just indulge in lust. There isn't a man born that doesn't desire to satisfy the one they love. Men endure frustration and angst as the potential for making love slowly fades over a lifetime in the face of conditioning that convinces him it won't ever happen.

Conscious admission of the lack paves the way for the fulfillment of the human race. Achievement of loving sex, only then, can unleash the full potential of love.

Do not avert your gaze because the word love is mentioned. This is not some pie-in-the-sky, desperate attempt to proclaim love as some, mysterious, mystical force that will save our existence. It is a hard-nosed look at what hinders the acceptance of the broader brushstrokes of a sentient, self-aware perspective and existence. Lust is the destructive foundation that forces a beastly existentialist perspective. The human physical act of love empowers the loving sentient perspective.

Mankind's humanity is fulfilled by men eliminating the undermining nature of undisciplined animal-like sex. The misconception is that our civility will somehow improve due to punishment of transgressions (e.g. legal systems, enforcement, etc) and education. We are not Pavlov's dog. We just act like it.

Integrity, honesty, and caring, etc. are inherent qualities of a sentient race whose self-respect remains intact. Teaching does not instill these qualities. The qualities are not developed through fear of punishment. They are the natural results of self-respect. All of these are assaulted, undermined, and defeated by the severe failure of self-respect due to the failure of sentient sex.

Systems of punishment are a childish approach to our problems. They are a form of sadomasochism, punishing ourselves for our sentient awareness (and failure). In a paranoid manner, we try to put a lid on the boiling cauldron of our distorted sentience. We never realize that we only prolong the assault in delusion as long as we accept the monkey.

Until remedied, we will remain a furtive creature. Women will remain subjugated and men will remain jerks unable to love. The sentient perspective of both genders are assaulted due to the ongoing delusion concerning the nature of sex and its fulfillment.

It is not intelligence or learning that will set us free. There are plenty of intelligent, well-educated jerks. Self-respect is undermined each time the most fundamental act of life is not fulfilled as the beast thrusts away in abandon.

The squalor of human misery is a sham, an absurdity. Our irrational 'nature' is nothing more than induced delusional reactions that defeat a fully sentient self-aware existence.

The ongoing assumption is that our dysfunction is natural, that sentience is the problem. This is clearly represented by our systems of rules and punishment. We have never even seriously considered that we could be good without taming and the threat of punishment. Trust and honesty is our natural state.

The dysfunction is understandable because we have been constantly immersed in the dysfunction of our sentient existence from the beginning. The process of realization is not simple. As you read this, you may very well balk. Conditioning may eat away at you to reject these insights. In the conditioning to avoid deep thoughts on the subject of sex, we act like a trained monkey. Pavlov's dog would be immensely proud.

We focus on the surface issues created and distract ourselves from that which can make us whole. All of the folly that we consume daily in our headlines are just the results, not the source, of our dystopia. We conclude that we have to fight our way through the results like an animal rather than just accept the grace of our sentient existence. It is a carousel of nightmares.

No education, training, or punishment can ever overcome the loss of self-respect provided by bestial rutting. Throughout the long millennia of our disturbed state of sentience, the worst case, most deluded, confused individuals remain brutish indeed. While it is displayed as hate for others it is, at its very heart, self-hate and frustration taking a delusional, fierce hold. Yielding to non-sentient, self-serving lust (not sex itself!) instigates it all.

Shortsightedness, due to our finite lifetimes, fools us into believing that our imbalanced existence is actually improving. The deceit becomes more intricate to dupe each new, more fully aware generation, while the suspicion that something is wrong continues to grow. Brutishness and unreason have not diminished. They just adapt. The turmoil will continue until we remove its source.

The stupefaction of humanity

The usual sexual experience is imbalanced. Before sentience, that was the common case and made sense. The limited scope of an animal has one overriding intention: propagate the species. Just impregnating the female is no longer enough for self-aware beings. Sex progressed, whether we like it or not. Our complex nature requires more. The lack drives men mad.

The experience of making love (i.e. both achieving emotional and physical fulfillment) has been mostly missing since our emergence into a sentient state. Because there are so many afflicted, it destroys the sentient character of the race. Learning to make love is not just a nicety. The fulfillment reinforces self-respect that is essential for a sentient perspective.

Awareness of the potential for making love is an attribute that distinguishes us from other animals. Success makes us human. Our inability to do so creates the brutish caricature of false bravado and pompousness portrayed by men to mask their frustrated feelings of emasculation. It is our most absurd, utter, and unnecessary failure. We stray further from sanity the longer it remains accepted.

Sentience brought into question something of such magnitude that our newly emerging awareness and intellect were confounded by its scope and defeated by its subtlety. The initial inability to overcome failure set in motion conditioning (brainwashing, if you will) that has caused us to avoid confronting the obstacle for millennia. Misdirection and outright deceit were developed in tandem with our emerging sentience to cope, resulting in complete confusion.

Our intellect was not ready to cope with what our awareness had made appallingly apparent. The many gifts provided by sentient self-awareness have, thus, been delayed by millennia. Brutishness is not a natural trait for our race. It is a throwback to our animal predecessors. We are far more than animals with a big brain. We remain untrue to our sentient nature.

Something so transformative as sentient sex was beyond our ancient ancestors' comprehension. They attempted to described it, and ended up distorting it more and more, in myths. The distortions have now reached the state that we are beginning to embrace the 'animal spirit' and fully accept the beast.

The conditioned acceptance of the unchangeable nature of bestial sex combined with the inexorable desire for sex, too often followed by failure, ensures feelings of despair and frustration, leading to acceptance of the selfish animal state.

The most common male sexual endeavor can be described as just relieving sexual pressure. The disturbing psychological consequences cannot be avoided. It is a sentient failure when the man only takes and the woman only gives sexual satisfaction. It inadvertently forces a selfish, bestial perspective on the man. The woman's emotional component is fulfilled by satisfying her mate. She is only humbled and frustrated by the lack of her own satisfaction, not destroyed.

The disastrous effects are only amplified due to men's inexorable desire for sex. It is not the lack of, or need for, sex that destroys a man. It is the lack of the satisfactory conclusion to the sexual engagement that undermines his manhood and destroys his humanity. It begins to ripple out as a species-spanning misogyny but has evolved into every corruption of our race. The complexity and interconnectedness of the intricacies of our delusions and corrupted spirit would fill a book.

Beginning with our earliest myths, the desire for a culprit has often exploited women as the scapegoat. The convoluted rationales required to justify the insanity of misogyny portrays the bizarre situation. Our avoidance of noting its source is telling.

The facade has become appallingly apparent over the last century as our intellect has become increasingly and uncomfortably aware. The final breakthrough has been approaching for centuries.

Men's aversion to the phrase making love is one of the most revealing and curious examples of our natural inclination towards honesty and honour. As long as men fail, they will continue to balk at using the phrase that they know they are not fulfilling. It is not a man's lack of desire to fulfill the woman that impedes. It is the lack of knowledge of how to do so.

Making love is the act of self-awareness rising above our animalistic past by engaging in sex in which satisfaction is equally shared. Sentient sex is only the outermost layer of the gift that nature and sentience grants. The more complex characteristics of an unimpeded sentient existence will only become fully apparent once the sentient perspective fully emerges in honesty to clarify.

We can easily complete the magnificent nature of sex in its ultimate, eye to eye self-aware form. Pleasure and emotional fulfillment can be provided for both while continuing to propagate the species as necessary. Sex is not a curse. Making love is not a curse. Sentience is not a curse. Fulfillment of man *and* woman is not a curse. Bestial enactment of lust is.

Learning to make love is the only answer. The way to do so must become common knowledge. This critical adjustment is entirely the man's responsibility and easily achieved. Our suppression of its importance is due to men's desperate attempt to avoid recognition of their failure that is only due to the conditioning to continue to fail.

Human sentient qualities are subverted by the substitution of animal lust for love. The brute characteristics of an animal deform our sentience and intellect leaving us in a lesser state in which we wreak havoc.

The abandoned search for the ability to last as long as desired to sexually satisfy a woman has held us hopelessly in check. It slowly turned us into a crude caricature of a fully sentient being. It is the only challenge we have ever blindly accepted as insurmountable and shunted aside with excuses and scapegoats. As our intellect and knowledge grew, our humanity diminished. All else follows.

Sentient attainment

We avoid the fullest expression of our sentient nature until we accept that self-aware sentient sexual expression is different. Taking this step towards becoming fully human highlights the difference between self-awareness and the beast, equality and misogyny, love and lust, making love and the beast's selfish sex.

Our nature, as a *fully* sentient race, is to be emotionally stable, rational, and disciplined. We achieve greatness once we accept the difference that can differentiate us from all of the animals that preceded us. Our sentience is attained through the inclusive, fulfilling sentient sexual expression of making love rather than indulging in the self-serving act of rutting like an animal. Nature freed our awareness to understand the compromised act of rutting. We must free ourselves from the underlying imbecilic instincts that withold the accomplishment.

If one scrutinizes the human experience closely, the necessity for goodness that self-awareness requires contrasts sharply with the chaotic, bestial, and sometimes cruel, rabid qualities displayed in our current subhuman condition. We are caught between the beast and the human. There is an underlying urge to do good, be good. Self-respect is how a cohesive self-aware sentient perspective maintains itself. A distorted self-aware perspective rationalizes its corruption and trains itself not to care. The befuddled beast remains as long as we rut like animals.

Discipline, reason, and emotional balance do not suggest numb, emotionless, or monotonic behaviour. They indicate a state uncluttered by deceptions and relieved of the resultant confusion and delusion. It is love rather than self-aggrandizement. It is joy rather than jokes. It is celebration of existence, rather than forced joviality and farce pompously, preposterously, and ashamedly endured in the face of misery. Life is not just an infinite jest.

The trouble that mankind endures comes down to the individual. As long as the individual is unsettled, deceived, and convinced of nonsense, so will mankind be. When the majority of individuals attain an emotionally stable state by retaining self-respect, the delusions tolerated by society will begin to dissipate. Mankind becomes human rather than a deluded beast.

Transformation

Humanity is an adolescent sentient race that has not yet attained its maturity. A mature sentient race would not endorse the childish nonsense that we so readily accept as our existence.

There are physical and emotional components to making love. In our current lopsided state, the woman experiences the emotional fulfillment of her mate's complete physical satisfaction while seldom experiencing the full physical satisfaction herself. This is the more stable situation. The man experiences the full physical satisfaction while the emotional fulfillment fails utterly in lack of the physical satisfaction of his mate. This is a devastating, destabilizing experience that hobbles self-respect and humanity.

The essentials of the myth of Pandora's Box that were so fabulously accurate suggest the ongoing procession of our dilemma. Some contingent of our earliest consciousness was unburdened enough to attempt to express the dilemma accurately. Some few were fully aware and honourable, but confounded. Then, the miserable situation began to chip away at our self-awareness and delusion built upon delusion.

As time progressed, the emerging inability to conquer the lack led to the embellishments that grew to malign women and sentient self-awareness. We became filled with delusion, frustration, and deceit that reflect the beast and continues to grow in its distortions. We continue to lose honour. Yet, the momentum to retrieve that goodness, the desire to achieve love, honour, and self-respect continues in the shadows.

In completing the self-aware sexual experience, we unleash the sentient perspective that contains our honour, self-respect, love, and our final attainment of something well beyond the beast. Yin and Yang become equal. We complete each other. This does not mean an end to our troubles, just an end to *self-induced* dystopia. Love is not a cure-all. It is a requirement for a sentient race to counterbalance its formidable intellect. As our intellect developed, the counterbalancing component of love was shunted aside through foolish shame. Pavlov's dog has reigned supreme in havoc.

Now, we can begin to move out from under the shadow of confusion that has haunted us and finally perceive a sentient perspective untarnished by the beast.

Perspectives

This is not a plea to love thy neighbor as he hammers you over the head. This is the realization that any member of a fully sentient race will not have the emotionally impoverished, witless desire to hammer any other member over the head. Non-sentient sex unwittingly generates an excessively selfish, vicious perspective for men and a distorted environment for the humanity.

When the sexual satisfaction of one partner is missing, the sentient perspective of both becomes disoriented. Engaging in the incomplete act of lust begins the deterioration of intimacy rather than its celebration and reaffirmation. That limits existence to an animal's perspective, while our sentient conscience and awareness continue to rebel.

Due to the convoluted conditioning, we have become subconsciously convinced that the sexual situation can never change. Men desperately seek full resolution while remaining convinced it does not exist. This continues to perplex our sentient awareness. Every aspect of our existence reflects the hopelessness and confusion that we endure.

We are too smart for our sentient nature not to note the situation. Yet, we still remain mired in the conditioning that defeats us. Most are just humbled by the situation. Some are utterly defeated. Others lose all moral compass as they irrationally exploit the situation selfishly or erode their sanity further by accepting nonsense to rule their lives. Our magnificence is utterly lost in the confusion.

The woman's satisfaction was not even a consideration in past millennia. A man's desperate, embarrassed rationalizations concerning failure ensured the thought process that women are only necessary for providing sexual relief. Any chance at a loving perspective was shot. Women's slow impatience with the obduracy of men has glacially slowly begun to change things superficially. But, only love-making can ever fulfill the situation.

The couple attempting satisfaction for the woman by any means is a rather recent development. While an improvement, anything less than eye to eye love-making remains an awkward caricature of what it should be. Confidence in enacting the eye to eye physical expression of love is an immeasurable improvement in the self-aware state. The common ability is essential to the flourishing of a fully sentient perspective. Still, satisfy the woman in any viable way in the meantime.

Providing satisfaction is the all-important physical display of sentient caring that clarifies and fulfills self-awareness. Adopting a caring attitude into the act of sex is a difference that no male of a lesser species can ever even contemplate. The mindless act of rutting overturns that sentient desire and relegates us to the untenable bestial state.

Eye to eye loving ensures self-respect, bolsters self-confidence, and reveals a sentient perspective. It frees the human, caring, perspective. Lust destroys even the glimmer of self-awareness and reduces us to an unsuitable bestial existence.

In the past, the option of making love and pleasing one's female mate was such a foreign concept that one insane suggestion was that the only way to be truly good was to do without. Right. Like that ever works out well or makes the slightest sense.

Another insane conclusion is that the disruptions we endure are the unfortunate consequences of sentience, the curse of awareness, the unavoidable sin for which we will always pay.

It is not willpower, education, punishment, some frilly philosophy or blind sermon that will improve our existence. They only further distort the situation. Only confidence in love-making releases self-respect and, thus, reason and emotional balance.

The bitter feeling that one will never fulfill the physical component of love is a devastating experience. It is thrown in one's face repeatedly, constantly, and maddeningly throughout a lifetime from puberty on. The bitter feeling is currently called 'attaining maturity', 'recognizing reality'. It is a state that becomes more destructive as it wears away sanity with age. Care, *for a sentient race*, is the rule, not the exception. It is unenforceable, unlearned. It flourishes naturally in a self-aware environment.

Unobstructed self-awareness invokes the sentient version of caring. Rutting relieves the animal urge for sex but compromises self-respect and, thus, intellect, caring, honor, and integrity, etc. In other words, a self-aware perspective. Lust inhibits humanity's development. It is the unwilling acceptance of and surrender to a impoverished, disturbed state. We will completely fulfill our sentient perspective once making love in an eye to eye tangle becomes the common expectation and result.

Men are physically driven to sexual release. It is a man's self-awareness that desires something more beyond sexual release. The conditioning whispers, "there's no hope" for his manhood to ever be more than a beast. How does one care or remain human in such a case? The desire begins to hide itself behind ludicrous bestial caricatures of manliness as failure is repeatedly and ashamedly thrown in his face for a lifetime.

It is impossible for a man's self-awareness to ever fully deny the desire for a woman's physical satisfaction. When a man achieves his own satisfaction in absence of hers, rationalizations and selfish tendencies insidiously creep in to pollute his world view. The vague belief that others can do better is devastating.

Conversely, consider it from a woman's perspective. It is nearly always true that the woman physically satisfies her lover. Self-awareness is never assaulted directly. Sentience remains tentatively in tact. She may be baffled, disappointed, frustrated, harangued, and abused, but never directly compromised by failure. Her spirit marches on.

The scope of the problem

Each time a man fails to satisfy his lover, he subconsciously questions his manhood. His drive for sex, though, never relents. The ramifications are vast. Blaming women for the incongruity of the sexual experience is only the tip of the iceberg. The subconscious rationalizations release a host of vituperativeness and paranoia.

It is not just one couple that suffers. This is essential in order to fully understand. It is clearly a lot of men that fail, by any estimate. The ability to last as long as desired may be a vanishingly small segment of men. Whereas the opposite should be the case. Any man *can* last as long as he pleases. Once his confidence and self-respect are retrieved, he can spend the time and effort to learn love-making in all of its nuances. He can then become a loving, fulfilling partner in the relationship rather than a brutal ruler in a kingdom of facade.

Making the situation more ridiculous and confusing, many men entertain the suspicion that the failure uncommon. How does a man deal with this feeling of personal failure and the suspicion that it is not common among other men? In whom does he confide? Whom does he dare ask to help him overcome what seems so personal, atypical, and embarrassing? It thoroughly distorts his view of life. Men's conditioning to avoid confidence-sharing of any kind is only one of many enduring characteristics attributed to men that are not inherent.

Men's first relief is realizing it is a common problem. The second relief is realizing it should not be the case for any man. It is a legacy, not a genetic result, of our animal heritage which is easily overcome by a sentient being using his intellect and a little discipline to overcome.

Even if a man has sought a solution in the past, the available answers have been inadequate, the misleading anecdotes disastrous. This leads to further despair, reinforcing the conditioning. The belief in failure has become remorselessly transfixed as unchangeable.

The little blue pill is not an answer. It does not soothe a man's ego to think that he needs help to be a man. It just deludes him into accepting the animal. The popularity of the little blue pill and the ample, useless literature on sexual performance suggest the gigantic extent of the problem. The evidence of widespread sexual failure and its importance to men is extensive. It must be reiterated, there *is* a solution! While any way in which to satisfy the woman is a vast improvement that eliminates the beast, only eye to eye loving fully realizes the human.

The worst conditioning of all is the desire to just look away, never consider the problem, never admit there is a problem and just accept things as they are. It remands us into delusion. We have endured this conditioning for more than three thousand years to our dismay and disruption.

Our dystopia is caused by the outward radiating self-hate in the forms of frustration, anger, cruelty, and despair due to the fundamentally skewed view that one's life is a hopeless failure. Just wait until you are dead. Things will get better then. Right.

Every man is born with the 'problem' that is not a problem for a sentient male. The solution is not dazzlingly complicated. It just deserves attention rather than disregard and neglect. The foolish concept of a man gritting his way to last just long enough seldom works at all and barely works in the best instances. It is attempting a beastly rendition to a sentient problem. The complex machinations of tantric sex or Kama Sutra to dress it up are not required, either.

Practical matters

By any account, our failure in love-making is insanity. It is that which brought us to our knees. If you go all the way back to the myths, you see the same inability to face the issue. The difference is that we now have the wit to overcome the limitation.

We have all participated in a sad charade for all these long millennia. All of the distorted, misleading, confusing misperceptions create an environment of delusion, deception, hopelessness, and despair. Dystopia.

We foolishly focus all of our attention on the blatant surface issues that plague our lives (e.g. geopolitical struggles, economies, religious schisms, crime, gossip, etc) and completely ignore the source that undermines them all. We tweak the systems (e.g. forms of government, societies, etc) as if the tweak represented some grand scheme to improve our state rather than an endless wheel of frustration. We ignore the fact that changes in the systems are only superficial. Humanity improves not at all.

The individuals, not the systems, are the relevant factor. The focus on surface issues and systems is only a distraction from the source that wreaks havoc. The systems will remain broken as long as the individuals comprising the systems remain hopelessly, desperately unfulfilled.

Every single one of us retains some measure of the magnificence that mankind can achieve. It is inherent in the self-aware state. We can sense it but never seem quite able to achieve it. We remain mired in a lesser state and accept our suffering, delusions, failure, and absurdity as inherent. The ramifications are profound. Our state of delusion increasingly affects every thought and action.

The disturbance within the individual creates a swindle that extends into every nook and cranny of our existence - and it's getting worse. We either accept our humanity or continue to devolve into a rabid beast. Our ever-increasing awareness of the parody, while avoiding its existence, has consequences. The distractions in which we revel always leave insane, unsatisfied cravings that we relentlessly chase in delusion. Nothing other than the potential for a loving relationship can ever fulfill our need.

The bizarre ways in which we view sex and the countless perversions, offenses, obsessions, cravings, outright lunacies and remorse surrounding sex provide the most potent proof that something is fundamentally awry with sex. Yet, we ignore it all as if it were to be expected because we are descended from animals.

The sexual context of our lives is the most troublesome part of our existence. Women are supposed to endure sex for the sake of creating new life and men endure their sexual failure because that's just the way it is. Sex, the very reason for our existence, is often viewed as if we would do better without it. How could this preposterous suggestion even exist? What should be a celebration of life is often nothing more than a complete and abject failure that burns our sentient perspective to ashes.

A lifetime is a long time to endure poor sex. Everyone suffers in such a case. The wear on a relationship is relentless. When the two necessary satisfactions are only achieved in a one-sided manner, sex becomes increasingly unfulfilling. That is bad news for relationships and our sentience. Even if a relationship survives, acceptance of the situation is devastating. The miserable, unfulfilled emotions extend outward into all of the interactions with others.

Some men may learn to struggle to last long enough, but few ever discover how to make it no struggle at all. As long as it is a struggle, the success is occasional and minimal, at best. Utter failure becomes more common as relentless feelings of despair, lethargy, and rationalizations set in. How can sentience exist in such a setting? The loving tangle, face to face, not only reaffirms self-respect but nourishes the relationship and all of life. The face to face loving tangle that fulfills is the most important sexual experience, if not the only one. Accepting the bestial act of rutting like an animal without satisfaction for both is the culprit that blinds our sentience. Any way in which to satisfy the woman is better than that.

The constant disappointment and disruption of lust invades every aspect of our existence. Sex should *and can be* the most extremely satisfying, fulfilling experience of life. It fulfills the relationship, the individual and, finally, humanity. When sex is completed in a sentient manner, it becomes a meaningful, loving part of life rather than an all-consuming obsession. As love-making becomes common, sex can become accepted as a well-adjusted, loving act rather than an obsession.

A forced situation

No outside force (e.g, legal systems and punishment) or influence (e.g. sermons, philosophy, cultural or peer pressure) can ever rid us of the frustration, disruption, and deception that lies deep in the heart of mankind. At best, these stopgap measures only suppress and conceal the real situation. They are not answers. They only distract from the unremitting disaster. We cannot fight our way out of the disaster. We emerge whole when we make love.

The pompous nonsense of politics and diplomacy, the insanity of constant war, murder, and other forms of violence, verbal or physical, are surface issues that only fester and worsen as long as the source of our insanity remains. They portray the actions of an animal boxed into a corner, lashing out in its stupor. It is a monkey-like caricature. The surface disruptions are not the cause but the results of our insanity. We incessantly attack the symptoms, not the disease.

The stopgap measures, the curbs, are a barbaric way in which to grit our way through a disturbed existence, lost somewhere between a beast and the human, rather than removing the primary disturbance wholly at its source and, thus, finally achieve a sentient perspective.

The articulated sentient description of life is embattled by these brute measures. We continue to invoke a haphazard and hazardous bestial description initially erected in stupor and deception. We have spent an inordinate amount of time refining and reinforcing the underpinning to all of these structures that can never be complete nor sound without a sound humanity. We have never faced our failure as an intelligent, fully self-aware race.

The subject has been way too painful for men to contemplate without an evident solution. *The solution is now available.* We no longer need to suffer, beg for a little blue pill, seek perversions of sexual desires that offend our consciousness, abstain, or indulge in less satisfying alternatives. Open acknowledgement of the ties between sexual failure and aberration will begin to constrain the expression of obsession and caricature. The common knowledge and practice of love-making will loose the avalanche of our sentient perspective.

Caricature

We must understand that we are far more than just a smart animal. Conditioning blinds us to the ongoing disaster of our failure to overcome. Nothing could ever condition us to avoid the act of sex. Instead, the disruption that begins in preconditioning becomes fully engaged as puberty is achieved. Sex is an overwhelming force that makes a caricature out of our existence as long as it continues in its maladapted form. It causes the mortification of men that runs counter to sentience and self-awareness. In that embarrassing bafflement, we developed a blindspot and substituted nonsense for reality.

Many of the characteristics attached to 'being manly' are an offensive caricature reminiscent of the beast. There would surely remain characteristics that distinguish a man from a woman but they have nothing to do with the portrayal of men as brutes or women as the subjugated gender that cares. Caring and self-respect are shared characteristics that should pervade both genders. A sentient Yin and Yang both become fully human.

Just as with men, a disabling situation is inculcated in women since birth through conditioning and begins to fully disrupt as they reach puberty. The offensive caricature of men and the miserable sex endured begin to have their effects on women, as well. It must be exceptionally baffling for women since only the results of the disruption are seen, but never clearly understood. It becomes a baffling matter of enduring an intolerable situation.

Retention of the individual's self-respect by engaging in loving sex is the only way to turn the tide for all, end the caricature of human life, and replace it with essential characteristics of sentience. It is the only force that can redirect our course away from the dystopia we have created and endured.

Honor, integrity, self-respect and a whole host of other redeeming characteristics are commonalities that *should* be expected as the defining characteristics of a sentient race and both genders. These characteristics lock Yin and Yang into a loving embrace beyond the scope of an animal, once released. The coherent, self-aware, sentient perspective can replace the bewildered caricature of a highly intelligent but witless beast. It is the high intelligence in the absence of a stable emotional outlook that creates a precarious and unfulfilling existence.

Sentience rising

This is all about men finally learning to lead the dance of physical love. This is about men bravely accepting the responsibility for success in the most intimate act by overcoming the insane conditioning we have all endured and, thus, release our sentience.

The essentials are simple enough to be passed on from father to son in conversation. Once they become commonly understood, they will finally make those father-son conversations meaningful rather than awkward. The awkwardness of those conversations is just another revealing aspect of the failure.

Making love is an art that we will desire to perfect. That is just the way it is with every human effort that is not scuttled due to baseless fear. We enthusiastically pursue improvement. The suppression of sex is quite remarkable. We have never hidden from any challenge other than achieving the loving nature of sex.

Humanity can gain a fully self-aware sentient perspective that need not hide in dark corners. The end result requires overcoming a vast array of deceptions that have proliferated due to the initial deceptions concerning sex. Uprooting these peripheral deceptions will not be easy or instantaneous. It can only begin once the facades of 'manliness' are overcome and self-confidence, integrity, etc become the predominant characteristics. The alpha male is a parody of sentient male confidence.

We become more fully aware and human, gain a sentient perspective, and put away the last remnants of the beast by finally accepting that sex for a sentient race is something more. The physical act of love is the greatest celebration of life for a fully sentient race other than life itself. Lying eye-to-eye in a fulfilled loving tangle is what it will take to begin to fully release the flood of sentience and care that has been absent. Lust is an obsession. Making love is transcendent. Rutting lust is for animals, making love is for humans.

Education, wealth, and wit are no talismans against depravity. The race's confidence in sentient sex is the only way to release (not instill or force!) the human qualities that are inherent in a sentient being. Only thus do we begin the journey towards a sentient perspective, wholeness, and further.

Moving forward

Just consider the fact that nature made sex in such a way that humans can gaze into each other's eyes. It is a stunningly prescient sign. Self-awareness is in the honest fulfillment eye to eye. Failure glares out at us in its absence and we look away.

Men desire sex, but more importantly, they desire to fulfill their partner. Only by fulfilling that desire do men fulfill their sentience. The bewildering, brutish, mindless madness in which we find ourselves lies in the gap between fulfilling both desires.

This is not just another philosophy suggesting how to change (or bear) the dystopian experience of human life by thinking in some specific manner that is counter to (or aligns with) everything we experience. This is a change to the experience of life itself that reorients us and fulfills our humanity. This is a transcendent change in the most fundamental experience of life. It transforms the sentient experience of life for the individual and relieves the dystopia. Imagination and pompous words with no inherent value were never enough. We can no longer cower in the darkness of our own deceptions and fear of failure.

The many otiose attempts at meaningless change, driven indirectly by subterfuge, only confuse our perceptions further and create madness. This is a real, pertinent change that is palpable by anyone that sheds the conditioning. Even those that retain the conditioning cannot avoid the sense that something is wrong, that we have been lying to ourselves. That sense has only been suppressed, not eliminated, leading to the current insanity.

This is a change of substance and clarification of perspective. It is a change in circumstances that liberates and transforms our perceptions, perspective, and human state.

The full panoply of a sentient perspective remains to be explored. A sentient perspective expands from a base of self-respect that is reinforced and maintained by confidence in life and the physical expression of love. Once released, the sentient perspective rescinds the limitations of our animal heritage. The fumbling way in which caring is currently expressed is reminiscent of the monkey, not a fully-formed sentient self-awareness.

It is striking that, when the loving relationship between two people is considered, the physical component is seldom mentioned as important. Our sentient sensibilities must openly acknowledge its significance. 'Irreconcilable differences' is a ruse.

What fails in the 'happily ever after"? What causes our dystopian existence? This "miserable *life*" or "cruel and unforgiving *world*" or "brutal *circumstances*" are the usual misleading phrases. They are wild misdirection. Replace "life", "world", and "circumstances" with "mankind" to come closer to the truth. "Sexual disaster" is the most honest substitution. Best will be when our perceptions no longer require a descriptive phrase for our dystopia as it no longer exists.

So far, we have built our existence on a foundation of sand. We have ridiculously retained the animal in us. We accept our nightmare as inherent and reject our magnificence. We propose that our magnificence and grace are only attainable through brute force. The absurdity of that proposal is incredible.

There are no inherent nightmares. The nightmares of our existence are transient and surmountable. Once men overcome their failure at sex, they retain the courage to face life as a sentient endeavor with self-respect. The nightmares end as the offensive, brutish perception of life is eliminated. Yin and Yang can finally come into balance.

The irony is exquisite. What can set us free is finally permitting the outcome that we have always desire most, a loving relationship. A relationship that is not built on angst and endured in misery that expands to make all other relationships fulfilling.

Just as ironic is that the source of our troubles that we so avidly avoid facing creates some, and exacerbates all, of the surface issues that we combat to no avail with every fiber of our being. The self-induced dystopia we endure should not exist. The list of ironies goes on. It permeates every aspect of our lives.

The non-sentient pontification that sex is bad is so erroneous as to be painful, so absurd as to be laughable. Our sages propose love is important and, then, denigrate its source. Loving sex completes us. It initiates a loving perspective. The ancient confusion between sex and rutting is understandable but no longer tolerable. Lustful rutting is the sexual model that the common animal engages in to assure procreation. The limited, beastly form of animal lust is destructive to sentience. It reduces us to an aberrant human state or promotes us to a aberrant animal state, whichever you prefer.

Reality becomes clear. We are *not* inherently disturbed. We have *misled* ourselves. We are only cursed by our unnecessarily limited ability at sex. We proclaim sex is bad and shameful. We are subconsciously convinced that we can do no better. The fact is that *lust* is bad for a *sentient* race. *Lust* is a shameful, inappropriate enactment for a highly intelligent, self-aware race. *Our intellect equips us for more* and rejects anything less. Loving sex is human, essential, and liberating.

The ages old proclaimed curse was embarrassingly mislabeled. The curse should have always been noted as lust, not sex, certainly not loving sex, not love. Our ancient ancestor's simpleton view did not distinguish as they bashed their way through life like an animal. Sex is not bad. Lust is bad. Loving sex is fulfilling. Lust becomes distorting and obsessive in its endless pursuit of something that never occurs, loving.

We need to learn and celebrate sex in its love-making, sentient form. We are bridled by our own confusion and conditioning concerning the subject. The skillful, sentient approach to sex, best termed as making love, can set us free. Sex itself is *not* bad. The animal form of sex performed by a self-aware being is a disaster. It misleads us away from cognition into blind destruction. Make love, not lust.

The accuracy of the term *making* love is incredibly insightful. The physical act of love is that which releases a loving state of mind in which a sentient perspective and love can flourish.

The disruption is real but it is not inherent. The issue and resolution are clear. Animals rut. Sentience recognize that there can be something more. Physical love enables the state of love. Love-making, well, ... makes love! It creates a loving perspective.

Long ago, we became aware of the injustice pertaining to non-sentient sex, lustful rutting. The injustice was poorly stated or misinterpreted in every case. Sex was proclaimed bad rather than selfish rutting. The complex nuances of sex baffled the limited capabilities of our ancient ancestors. The best they could do was make vague references that something was amiss. The worst initiated blindness, repudiation, and vile acceptance of the beast.

Loving sex is the foundation of an egalitarian existence for a sentient, sex-based race. It engenders the higher form of sentient caring called love, and fulfills a self-aware sentient race.

Full understanding

There is no reason left for any man to avoid becoming a great lover. Relief and fulfillment begins once a person becomes convinced that they can partake in the excellence of love-making. The paradigms of nonsense rapidly begin to fall away.

Take the bold step and learn (or assure that you receive) the fulfillment of physical love for your own sake. If past puberty, the conditioning has begun to distort perceptions in earnest, but that can fade. Perceptions begin to peer beyond the fog of delusion as self-respect begins to flourish. Honor and integrity are fed by self-respect. As enough people become fully sentient, self-respect can flourish and humanity can transcend.

The sooner men unburden themselves, the sooner humanity can respect itself and move on. It is not some vague potential distant, future, enhanced animal state. It is here and now and fully human. The potential ascendence into a fully human state is swift.

Look around. Is this a race that respects itself today? The nonsense and brutality we tolerate is offensive, preposterous, bestial, and everywhere. The bogus claim that dystopia is in our nature is the most destructive distortion. Absurdity is not part of a sentient creature's doom. Our dystopia is nothing more than a ludicrous monkey in its stupor struggling as it browbeats itself.

Our current state is a destructive, bizarre, incomprehensible parody of self-awareness that circumstances and conditioning created. Perceive the rare gem ensconced.

Human beings adapt. That is one of our most powerful traits. Yet, we have never adapted to the most wonderful aspect of a sentient existence. The lack of adaptation turned a potentially caring, loving race into an emotionally unstable, self-centered, obnoxious, machiavellian brute that destroys its own existence.

Whenever a man acts like an animal rutting for its own pleasure, we are diminished and the animal caricature is reinforced. Fulfilled, loving sex produces an unobstructed, loving, confident perspective. Sex, for a sentient being, is fulfillment of one's mate *as well* as oneself. Ingrained confidence to do so transforms the race.

Lust carried forward into a sentient existence was the original mistake. It is not a sin but an inherited trait from our animal predecessors that does not suit sentient existence. Neither sex nor sentience is a curse laid on mankind. Lust is only an obstacle to the consummation of a sentient perspective that is hurdled by achieving the physical enactment love.

Every man that breathes desires to fully satisfy his woman. The solution is now known, described, and easily available. From there, we can continue to improve and elaborate the sentient perspective and love-making and begin to address all distortions caused by its absence. Mankind relieved of the burden of failure can fulfill itself. The chapter on Techniques And Considerations in the book, *Sentience,* thoroughly addresses the issue of love-making and the debilitating instincts. The 2019 revision is preferred as there are many refinements and further insights but the essence of resolution doesn't changed. We should expect continuous cycles of improvement in our ability to make love. It is that important.

We evolve as we become a race that fulfills the physical aspects of love. A sentient perspective can begin to flourish. A disciplined, humanity-centric (opposed to self-centric) existence becomes achievable. Humanity, as a whole, benefits. Humanity becomes human, civilization becomes civilized, society becomes sane, Yin and Yan fulfill each other, and the universe becomes a challenge, not a paranoid threat.

Yin and Yang need no longer remain distorted. We can overcome the confused, brute animal that has only the slightest awareness of its breathtaking potential. We can proceed into the grace and poise of a fully sentient self-aware experience.

A refinement of perspective concerning the most important activity of existence, our raison d'etre, can begin to bring our sentient self-aware perceptions into full alignment with reality. To be clear, everyone needs to know that loving sex is possible.

When we learn the skill of making love, we become something more. The much broader aspects of a sentient perspective become apparent and flourish as it ripples through the population. The incomplete insights from Spiritualism to Transcendentalism, and Chivalry to Flower Power, all sensed that there is something more. That now culminates in the sentient acceptance of physical love. The Theater of the Absurd describes the barren, existential alternative.

Theater of the Absurd

In our recent past, many were baffled by the surrender of the Flower Power generation to the miserable and corrupt conditions they had initially, adamantly, and instinctually rejected. Surrender was immediately assured by the unwitting, unsatisfying proclamation of Free Love.   Free Love is not love.   It is undisciplined lust given free rein with the best intentions and the usual calamitous results.

When lust no longer clouds humanity's perspective, mankind will minimize, if not eliminate, its inclination to take selfish advantage.   Selfish behaviour is reinforced every time a man takes his pleasure without reciprocation. It insinuates its way into every aspect of his perspective.   At best it leads to a tentative approach to life that is stunted and defeatist. At worst, it becomes a brutish, animalistic caricature reflecting the man's unacknowledged, therefore vicious, self-centered feelings of emasculation.   Distortions accrue for both genders, only the manifestations differ due to the differences in perspective.

We have remained in an unsuitable animal state for many millennia and we must finally recognize that fact. Self-awareness requires more than being a smart animal.   Self-awareness becomes unobstructed when we overcome the indulgences of the animal that blind us and cause us to avoid the mirror.

Mankind itself is our worst blindspot. We have avoided turning our discerning gaze on mankind itself in an incoherent attempt to avoid admitting to the disruptive situation. We have justified and accepted the insanity of our existence for too long rather than admit that lust is inhuman in the erroneous belief that we can do no better.

We cannot avoid sex.   So, instead, we avoid a close inspection of mankind and its bestial enactment of sex, blurring perceptions and corrupting our perspective, as it continues. This avoidance of self-inspection has bidden us to shrug off the havoc that we cause and accept it as our essential nature. Now, we can reject the distortions to self-awareness. Clear self-awareness can be considered an internal guidance system. It guides from within.

Resorting to external forces, such as fear of punishment, peer pressure, sermons, or philosophical views only confounds the situation further.   We are *not* an untrained monkey.   That depicts the breadth of our failure. We are far more different from the monkey than we ever imagined. Self-awareness is different.

Sexual failure creates an irresistible internally generated force that unwillingly grants access to the animal and dims self-awareness. The access that begins with early conditioning becomes fully granted in the presence of failure at puberty. The growing internal admission of failure confirms the delusions, bids the animal entry, and continues to degrade the view in the mirror.

The prospect of sexual fulfillment changes the situation radically. An emotionally stable perspective that retains self-respect resists the offensive bestial intrusions. Resistance to behaviours of the beast becomes stout, if not insurmountable, when the beast is never granted entry. The beast we accept is less than the human potential that our self-awareness justifies.

The worst rationalizations and justifications of the selfish (i.e. lustful) desires occur once brute nature is conceded and self-awareness is abdicated. No satisfaction in life exists once the brutish state is accepted. The selfish perspective of the beast deludes the sentient being into endless cravings that never fulfill.

A internal moral compass, not external moral stricture, is required. Mankind cannot be subdued by stories, pontifications, beliefs, or punishment. It must be freed of delusion and deception. We overcome the animal though internal orientation rather than inept attempts at external guidance from another delusional sentient being.

Offensive excuses that "we are only human", "it is the expected behaviour", "it is the only way to get ahead" do not ring true when an internal moral compass provides guidance. The lies told and accepted by the animal are no longer acceptable. Those first lies created and accepted to accommodate inept sexual engagement by a befuddled self-aware animal flourish and expand to encompass all of life. Self-worth is extinguished. We become more skillful liars with each new generation as meaning continues to elude us and evidence of our insanity develops further. The delusion becomes more self-destructive for the race and the individual as we proceed in delusion.

Corruption of the sentient perspective has gained a lot of headway. It has fanned out from its initial provocation to invade every aspect of our existence. It will take time to overcome all of the ramifications of the corruption that continues to spread.

It seems incomprehensible that such a tiny aspect of life as sex could have such a powerful impact, but its persistent leverage is enormous.

All of life begins with the relationship between man and woman, literally. Our existence begins there. Our societies, viewpoints, and progress begin there. Sanity or depravity begins there.

How does one measure dignity and honour once self-worth becomes compromised from within? Self-awareness is conditioned to look away from itself due to the sexual conundrum. It then distracts itself further with rumours, gossip, and headlines that confirm our depravity.

Conversely, how could a fully formed sentient creature that has not been stripped of its self-respect and humane qualities grovel in the depths of depraved misery or greed? It becomes incomprehensible.

Our desire to distract attention towards the machine, the systems of mankind, the surface issues rather than the source of our troubles is due to the fixation to look anywhere but where the problem really resides. We look everywhere else without answers or fulfillment. As the conditioning recedes, you will look around in shock at the breadth of nonsense that mankind has tolerated.

Take a moment to ponder this. What humans fear most is mankind itself. Pause (really!) and think hard on this incongruity!

Mankind has been burdened with misery and confusion since the beginning due to the failure of our sentient state. We have thoroughly numbed ourselves into a non-sentient condition, though it becomes increasingly difficult as our sentient awareness progresses. The rationales must now work overtime to delude our perspective as the potential for meaning, as well as our dystopian circumstances, become glaringly apparent.

Dystopia is a disgruntled animal state endured by a self-aware race that is no longer just an animal. We lash out at each other and the misery of 'an unjust world' because we have failed to overcome the distortions to a sentient perspective.

We are really good at tolerating misery. That doesn't mean we should. We continue to prance around on the stage of the Theater of the Absurd. We accept the stage of the absurd as our very existence (pun intended).

The stage

The Theater of the Absurd and the concept of existentialism that it represents, describes our predicament exceptionally well. Human existence has no meaning or purpose - as long we continue to delude ourselves into remaining an animal and avoid the elephant in the room. We perceive the purposeless surface machinations and manipulations of mankind by mankind and, thus, conclude that we are a dystopia-ridden brute *by nature*. We accept brutish transgressions as human and our existence remains absurd.

Still, we sense the unattained potential. We grasp the potential but not the substance. The potential is not absurd nor is its realization. The potential is best seen in some children that remain untainted by fully deluded role models for a little while. The current view suggests that the innocence of youth is a delusion that must be abandoned in order to attain maturity. Innocence is equated with naivety and gullibility. The innocence of youth depicts just how quickly our transcendence can begin. It is not the slow progress of a beast slogging its way out.

Innocence is the courage of sentience that is finally abandoned in dismay and delusion. It is no wonder that the Theater of the Absurd developed during the insanity of WWII. Has our existence gained more meaning or become less combative or deluded since? The instigating thugs of WWII are never far away.

The maturation process of our sentience is regressing. The predicament in which we remain ensnared makes existence more absurd as our awareness becomes more discerning. We increasingly become disoriented as we desperately ignore the evidence thrown in our face. We become more and more absurd.

The inevitable peak in absurdity, without the necessary counterbalancing force, is returning, once again. There is only one way off the stage. The surrender to lust as a substitute to making love obfuscates the exit door, abandons the will, and relegates us to the vile state of a deranged animal.

The race that fulfills its self-awareness is not absurd at all. Life becomes sentient, fulfilling, and meaningful. Love exists in the fulfillment of self-awareness as we attain a sentient perspective.

Of Absurdity

A specious argument rages that was created in the delusions of the beast. There is no winning side because each side argues from the same initial misconception. The hamster continues to run on its wheel. All sides argue their own brand of nonsense that benefits their own position. Every side howls in the dark. The most pompous, self-important justify their own selfish corruption. The bickering becomes more ridiculous and delusional with each rendering. It is the context of the argument that fails utterly. It makes the critically mistaken assumption that mankind is no more than a smart monkey.

The crux of the argument is whether the monkey can be trained or not and whether anyone cares. Most don't care. Selfish desires rule above all. Delusions run rampant within the argument. The assumption is that bestial behaviour is inherent, so just choose between the various evils. Our sentience is deemed no more than a curse that we must suffer through. Human potential is considered a distant goal that will never be fully attained or a complete delusion. Participation in the argument binds the bestiality of mankind.

One view is that there is something more if we can only somehow educate the beast out of us. This view is most accepted in the desperate aftermath of war. Another view accepts the beast as the best we will ever attain and, thus, acts out the part. This is most accepted leading up to war. These two views are the arguments of the dreamer and the pragmatist.

The fundamental problem is acceptance of the premise that we are an untrained monkey. The argument relies on acceptance of mankind mimicking Pavlov's dog. One side wishes to train the dog. Another thinks no training will help, so just jump in and have your way. Others wish to just put the dog out of its misery. Some mimic the dog very well. All sides blind themselves to nonsense and inconsistencies in their own arguments as they settle for a beast's compromise in the assumption that we are only animals. The wheel spins and humanity doesn't change at all.

The argument is currently flaring in the manner that it has repeated throughout our history as the angst of mankind, once again, reaches its inevitable peak of instability. As the argument flares, the usual result is rivers of blood. The manipulation of the many by the few most pompously deluded individuals triggers fury and blood-letting. The pompous justify their position in arrogance, stupor, blindness, and selfishness. The beast is confirmed as the befuddlement leads us closer and closer to vast destruction.

Absurdly, the call for application of force is always to be applied to those with a different government, perspective, lifestyle, other distinguishing characteristic or the lack of resources to sidestep punishment. The meek are not even a consideration.

Useless outside force applied to the selfish monkey is the failed substitute for liberation of the self-respect that mankind's self-awareness requires. We don't gain self-respect through punishing transgressions (or avoiding them). We just tread water and eventually drown in the muck of remaining a beast.

The argument never finds an answer because of the blatantly ignored elephant: fulfilling sex is required for sentience to flourish and the beast to be vanquished utterly. The erroneous precondition of the argument is that we can only fight our way out of the muck. It is absurdly mislabeled as recognizing reality.

As long as the premise is that mankind is an untrained (or untrainable) beast, mankind's attainments fail utterly. Once the premise is discarded and the importance of becoming truly human is accepted, we can immediately begin to transcend the animal.

The brute is a transgression, regression of self-awareness. The magnificent creature is sadly mistaken for an untrained monkey. Many pompously suggest that they are willing to turn the other cheek, which they never do. It would be pointless, anyways, without the perspective that mankind is *inherently* a loving creature that should have no rabid desire to lash out and strike another's cheek. Love also cannot be forced.

The phrase 'perceptions are reality' highlights the delusion. It justifies all of the distorted perceptions. A better phrase would be 'all perceptions of reality are not created equal'. Self-aware perceptions are radically different from those of an animal. Submitting to the beast destroys the human perspective, and self-awareness. Perceptions that indulge the beast inherently negate self-awareness in its distortions of a self-aware reality.

The worst, most dangerous viewpoint is proudly embracing the "animal spirit" in selfishness, and to hell with the future. "It's all about me" cries of the beast. That is the fully deranged, final brute state we will finally, fully attain if we don't change course and learn the workings of a loving relationship.

All sides have been willing to loudly argue their faulty view ad nauseam. Emphasis on 'nauseam'. Emphasis on the animal.

The necessary clarification that ends the argument is the awareness that we *are* a magnificent creature that never corrected its course. No future tense required. The fork in the road is abrupt.

Liberating self-respect enables self-awareness which releases emotional stability and reason. The deranged beast is overcome. Mankind achieves balance and stability by attaining sentient sexual competence, not by brutishly bearing the misery and dystopia induced by beastly lust. Furtiveness is not our natural inclination.

We are not predisposed to being a brute. We are enthralled into a brutish state by the disruption of the sentient perspective *and* our witless acceptance of it. We are an elegant, graceful race that occasionally, vaguely suspects the fact as it glances in the mirror of self-awareness.

We were gifted with hyperawareness and intelligence. We have been burdened with the unfortunate baggage and perceptions of our animal heritage. To embrace the former, we acknowledge and overcome the latter. Perceptions must match a self-aware reality.

The clarity instills a steadiness of character that is missing. Rational engagement radiates from that clarity just as hate, prejudice, and misery emanate from our failed, frustrated, blinded state today. Self-respect opens the door to a reasoning, emotionally stable existence. Sexual failure slams the door shut.

Arguing to love thy neighbor as he bashes you over the head will never get us there. Every man for himself will never get us there. Forced kindness is not enough. Brutish behaviour, no matter how it is fluffed up, is surrender and retreat.

The base assumption of the animal is displayed in every aspect of our disturbed existence. Worse, as long as the untrained monkey is the base assumption, the brute and the golden calf will win out. We must finally recognize that the brute is only a legacy, not the existence that our potential justifies. Overcoming the brute is not some distant, vague goal to be attained somewhat in some distant future.

Tinkering

We endlessly tinker with the systems and societies of mankind, central tenets of the grand absurd argument, in futile attempts to make a significant change to our circumstances. It is no more than the fascinated, exhausting distraction with the endless wheel of surface issues and antics of nonsense.

The systems do not need fixing. The people do. We'll never know what systems are sound until humanity is sound. The individuals that populate the systems, cultures, societies, and institutions are broken from the highest levels to the lowest. It's just that those at the highest levels are the most dangerous and, in their pomposity, are the ones that lead us right over the cliff as they nimbly avoid all punishment. They always ludicrously laud their successes and never take responsibility for the worst failure. They just look around in bafflement as it all goes wrong and comfort themselves that they did the best they could.

The beastly traits are brute relics that do not belong in a sentient, self-aware human being. We know it and the incongruity baffles us. So far, we have just accepted the disaster and failure of mankind as the monkey mimics what it believes it must be like to be human.

Our existence needs to proceed beyond the ongoing animal's stupor from which it all began. We ignore the obvious with profound anxiety and indulge the remnant of bestiality, thus obscuring the human in the mirror. We don't think because we have learned to block one disturbing thought.

By neglecting the transcendent state of sentience, we reduce our goals to curtailing the worst nightmares of the beast. Only tinkering with the systems, surface issues, and the mind of mankind is blind nonsense that eventually leads to utter failure.

The source of our troubles lies within the heart of the individual, not mankind's constructs or intrinsic qualities. We cannot legislate, shame, preach, or punish the demeaning traits out of the individual. The beast remains and only retreats into furtiveness under such conditions or proclaims itself loudly and proudly in the utter stupidity leading up to conflagration. Punishment only makes sense to a beast. It is not needed in absence of the beast. It just continues to drag out the damage in delusion. It is the impetus to poorly mimic beastly behaviour that must be excised. The beastly traits are completely foreign once the sentient, self-aware human retains its self-respect.   In the meantime, keep punishing away, until we become human.

In the absence of resolution, we have ignored our real dilemma.   The source of our problems and the remedy are now clear.   It's time to get on with it.   The beast must be left behind completely.   We dare not dawdle any longer.

Only by attaining our full, undeceived sentient perspective can we ever eliminate misogyny and sexism and, at least, *substantially* reduce the brutishness, racism, nihilism, narcissism, avarice, corruption, combativeness, violence, sociopathy, misanthropy, and social anxiety that we endure.   We will also never express a rational thought until we attain it.

Punishment does not produce the important changes necessary and no philosophy overcomes.   The former only suppresses and confirms the bestial behaviour.   The latter only analyzes the beast within its delusion.

The beast continues to rule.   The offensive traits are at least as evident in the rich as the poor, in the educated as the illiterate, the sanctimonious as the impious.   From prudishness to bestial degradation of women, it all fits.   In our current delusional state, the beast wins.   We must look in the mirror and eliminate the overridingly dominant source that releases the beast.   Our offensive behaviour can become an exception rather than the rule.

Emotional turmoil and unreason continue to gain inertia. Acceptance of the 'animal spirit' increases as we continue to convince ourselves that we are nothing more than a beast with little or no inherent redeeming value.   That is the final state of the distorted bestial reality that displaces a sentient perspective.

The brutish, combative, offensive, and self-serving behaviours that the source of our trouble encourages are so common that they are accepted as our fundamentally flawed nature.   They are, in fact, no more than lingering artifacts that we carried forward from our very, very confused and very, very ignorant ancient ancestors mimicking the untrained monkey.

Don't look for glory in our ancient ancestors.   Look for the glory in you.   Our ancient ancestors taught us delusions.   How could we possibly think that our ancient ancestors knew more, understood more than us?   We accept all of this nonsense rather than ever acknowledge the unnecessary sexual failure and frustration endured by so many men.   In the face of this awareness of our true potential, it becomes an offense against nature, humanity, and our future to continue.   The transition to achieving our humanity can be rapid indeed.

We've gone through revolution after revolution and espoused seemingly thoughtful nonsense over the millennia never changing anything of import as the monkey stumbled along. Mankind still abuses and takes advantage of mankind, no matter what form of government, legislation, rule, enforcement, religion, culture, or philosophy is imposed. We dress it up nicely, dream of better days (in past or future), suppress and punish the urges of those without power, ignore the aberrant behaviour of those with power (how much more monkey-like could we become?), as well as the underlying disruption, and carry on. The delusions multiply and the lies trip more easily from the tongue as we erode further into the beast and accept the animal spirit that is failure.

A new form of government (as an example) is proclaimed by some as the answer. They convince themselves that, once the shiny, new form of government is in place, it will solve all of our problems. They proclaim we have finally reached a better state.

The 'animal spirit' eventually begins to adapt. Weaknesses in the system are found. The cracks and loopholes are enthusiastically identified and exploited by the most deluded individuals that rationalize our deranged state for their own benefit with little or no regard for citizens or country, much less the full extent of humanity. For a beast, this tinkering with the animal's rules is justified. They are just an animal's rules, anyways.

The ways in which to manipulate the system become more evident and abused as time progresses. We then look on at the supposedly wonderful new system in befuddlement.

Or, as Frédéric Bastiat said, "When plunder becomes a way of life for a group of *men* (beast would be a more accurate term) in a society, over the course of time they create for themselves a legal system that authorizes it and a moral code that glorifies it." We are good at describing the flaws of the animal while never perceiving the human. We tinker.

The upheaval to the government system reaches its inevitable peak and wreaks deranged havoc. Enough blood is eventually spilled that the constituents finally right themselves, once again, to the extent that the underlying delusions allow.

In the aftermath of the soul-wrenching destruction, a ludicrous detailed inspection of the 'pertinent' surface issues occurs. This is followed by the inevitable proclamation of some wonderful new system to take its place and solve our problems that, once again, eventually fails. Ad nauseam. The human race does not improve one iota.

It is worth noting how often sex, in the form of lust, is used to corrupt. Lust, not the fulfilling act of making love, is used to convince people to abandon all moral *strictures*. It becomes a tool for the corrupt to extend corruption to others. It is not sex itself that degrades. It is the abandonment to self-serving lust. It is a man taking pleasure while providing little of real value in return.

Lust is a selfish act that encourages a selfish persona. It can corrupt the woman's perception of value, as well, by substituting some bauble for the inevitable lack of satisfaction that she has learned to expect. It degrades the ego. Lust becomes the acceptable practice as we succumb further to the animal spirit.

The corrupt know this game very well. No one has ever realized the converse because the truth of making love has remained virtually unknown. At best, it is vaguely sensed while failure continues. Making love is the one aspect of our lives that rejects the game and alleviates the absurdity in our existence. It is the one portrayal of sex not acted out on the stage of the absurd. It refutes making a bestial game out of sex and life.

Sex equated with lust suggests just how absent love-making is from consideration. Lustful rutting and sex are deemed interchangeable. Making love is not even a consideration. The act of making love creates no degradation. Sex is not bad. Lust is. We know the term love-making but refute its real meaning.

Men take and women give. This describes lustful sex as well as everything concerning our disrupted existence.

Consider the usual situation. A man says he loves a woman. It begins to dawn on him that he cannot physically satisfy his lover. His thoughts, his 'love', and his life, begin to fall apart. All of life begins to pall. Bitterness and angst begin to reign.

Accepting the failure diminishes. Avoiding the incomplete act diminishes. Attempting to find other solace diminishes.

Some men thrust with no concern for the lack of the woman's pleasure. He attempts to rationalize the act to allow his continued sexual relief and unintentionally accepts a selfish mindset and the beast. This eventually leads to anger, offensive behaviour, and a willingness to wreak havoc, a caricature of man.

Another way is some level of honest acceptance of the failure, rather than the thorough rationalization and blindness. This ensures eventual despair and feelings of defeat. Sensitivity is maintained while the spirit is destroyed in a different manner.

Some way out of this maze of insanity has been constantly and desperately sought to no avail. Our sentience has always subliminally screamed at us that it is not the sentient way as we gaze into, or avoid, each other's eyes. Our undistorted, sentient view hinges on the physical act of love. Only in fulfillment of love-making do we find our way out of the maze. Self-awareness requires that we learn the art of physical love that precedes and empowers all other aspects of love.

In the absence of the ability to make love, life's overriding command for procreation leaves us with the crippling alternative of surrendering to bestial lust or accepting a barren existence.

Why do so many couples have sex seldom or not at all? Lust is unfulfilling. In the absence of physical and emotional satisfaction for both, stress builds as the allure of sex wanes. A long term relationship filled with mutual respect and love becomes virtually impossible. With the miserable, bestial enactment of lust, the subconscious belief becomes that life is meaningless and a sufferance in the hopeless acceptance of the beast. The desperation creates the bizarre thought that, because this life is so miserable, we should expect it to get better *after death*. Right.

The ancient proclamation that sex is bad and only good for making babies is a futile attempt in our stupor to provide resolution that fails utterly. It is similar to the brute, bestial approach of Solomon cutting the baby in half. We only gain a rational, sentient perspective concerning life, sentience, and existence by making love and refuting everything concerning lust.

The magnificence and nobility of mankind is continually attempting to break out. It is often seen in youth, crushed by puberty, and utterly destroyed as the constant wear over a lifetime finally acknowledges failure. Youthful attempts at visualizing our magnificence succumb to the growth of misconceptions and the erosion of character into absurdity of confusion as one ages.

We need no longer cling to an abstract description of love without the substance. It is time to wake up to our humanity.

Inclusion

We are all connected by our humanity. Or, at least, we should be. So, where do the feelings of alienation, solitude, and isolation come from? As we discount the individual, the focus on humanity's surface turmoil creates a bewilderingly complex view. It begins to simplify once we focus on the most prominent source of an individual's insecurities, aberrations, and paranoia.

All of the barriers that have been erected over the millennia between subsets of humanity can finally begin to be dismantled as the primary barrier to inclusion and acceptance is removed and mankind's self-confidence makes its debut. All of the superficial divisions of mankind begin with the barriers erected between Yin and Yang. This portends the solution, a way forward.

Men's feelings of sexual failure cause havoc, disorienting the emotional state of the individual and the race. The upsetting suspicion that failure is a rare occurrence among other men exacerbates feelings of paranoia causing alienation and social isolation. With the lack of self-confidence, fear grows that others may not have the problem. Any differences in others become threats. The lack of self-respect, self-confidence, and self-worth in the individual has become reflected in the human race.

The misperceptions regarding the failure that men encounter act as a barrier to their openness. The failure is so deeply hidden across society that the man's character rebels against revealing his perceived failure. It eventually becomes cloaked in ludicrous behaviour to compensate. Avenues of open expression become barricaded. Men begin fearing any differences detected in others. Men become a caricature of confidence. Even women feel the effects. The disorientation suffocates. Any attempts at inclusiveness are snipped before they bloom.

Many sad caricatures of manliness have become accepted as the natural traits of men. We must overcome the source that causes the insane posing of the male gender in order for the human race ever to accept itself. Retention of the self-respect with which we are all born can allow humanity to advance towards inclusive self-awareness. Confidence and self-esteem can replace the feelings of failure and self-hate that are buried so deeply. Inclusion, rather than isolation, can become common once paranoia due to sexual failure is no longer a factor.

Self

As sentience first developed our spirit was still innocent, vivacious and whole, though little wit was yet available. Love became eloquently defined before the full insidious awareness of failure took complete control. Love has since worn into a word with little meaning in its daily use. Rather than expanding into the loving situation it should be, we became mired in delusions that befuddled the whole concept of love into a phrase without context.

Our burgeoning knowledge and intellect become increasingly dangerous in the absence of empathy, compassion, and conscience. Love increasingly becomes considered a weakness and delusion rather than essential to a sentient existence as life wears on and our existence strays further. Its lack ensures our dystopia. In its absence, the animal continues to rule our existence rather than the human. Animal stupor in the presence of human intellect is dangerous. Emotions are important. It is stunted emotions that fail mankind. Love fills in the picture. Physical love initiates it.

Blind idolization of science makes the concept of love seem even more quaint. Science is important and teaches us to question critically and perceive much about the universe. Critical observation of the universe or our beastly antics, though, is not enough to resolve our dilemma. We must turn and look deeply and critically in the mirror. Our scientific learnings are only helpful if we don't destroy ourselves with its beastly implementations and use or, conversely, ignore the insights in beastly hubris.

Self-love, particularly in men, has been virtually non-existent. Self-love for women has been obscured and downtrodden. The potential remains present in women but is often nearly distorted completely out of existence.

It is said that one must love themselves in order to love another. That may sum up this book and the interconnections between love, sex, self-awareness, and goodness better than anything else. "Love thy neighbor as thyself". Great idea. It is the latter portion of that phrase that is all-important and missing. We may finally be able to achieve that phrase in an all-encompassing manner. Mankind can love itself, surprisingly.

The words self-love and self-respect may be interchangeable. Certainly, one cannot exist without the other.

Radiate

The horrid acts of mankind and our dystopian existence are not the end game for mankind. It is just that without self-love, mankind continues to justify its sadomasochistic, self-destructive, dystopian existence and blames it on sentience. Self-gratifying existence is a beastly rendition. You should feel duped.

We can learn love and become fully human rather than tolerate our misery and each other in a brute existence. This universe certainly holds challenges, but mankind itself should not be our primary challenge. Sentience is not the obstacle. Our biggest concern need not be mankind's self-induced dystopia.

The mental and emotional state of the individual radiates outward influencing the human race through its everyday interactions. Retention of self-respect can unleash a growing avalanche of affection, care, and empathy to stabilize the human race. Does that sound farfetched to you? It is much easier to accept the dystopia and the radiations of frustration and misery that cause it than accept our own humanity. The conditioning to do so is that strong. Just open your eyes. The dystopia is a dodge.

The expansion of reason and stable emotions is as natural as the tumbling of the dominoes of self-awareness that nature has placed so well. They have been slowly tumbling for ages. We can finally tip over the all-important domino that has been teetering for at least a century. The remaining dominoes will tumble along the chain of our humanity with little effort.

We *should* be able to love all (reminiscent of The Hard Rock Cafe's motto ;~j ... Let's not get started on the link between the blues and sexual failure). When people can trust themselves to be stable, honourable, and act with reason, they make the tentative attempt to trust others to do the same. When the attempt to trust others is commonly reciprocated, trust and virtue can flourish. "Love thy neighbor as thyself" finally works. The final stage is trust in mankind to do right by itself. It starts with trust, based on fulfillment, in the relationship between Yin and Yang. At that intersection lies our ascendence or destruction.

Mankind can finally begin to transcend the state of an aberrant, furtive, highly intelligent and dangerous beast. A sentient state of inclusion, reason, and emotional balance can flourish in the presence of self-fulfillment and the resultant confidence in life. The facade of differences and divisions which now alienate us, one from another, can begin to retreat. Dystopia can fade as the contrary emotions that currently radiate outward due to self-hate vanish.

The self-love of the human race will take awhile to radiate throughout the race's consciousness. Self-hate is difficult to admit and confront. Bad sex even more so. Self-love begins with men fulfilling themselves in the only way possible. It slowly displaces the disillusionment, frustration, and aggravation that radiate outward. Women's fulfillment and release is contingent on men finally overcoming the burden that has held them back for so long. Yin and Yang can finally fulfill each other.

Love's very nature is bold indeed. It is exceptionally bold and courageous while it is an unusual occurrence. Women should know this in the depths of their hearts and souls. They have lived through the challenging situation always. The boldest women that retain love without confusion, blame, or remorse are remarkable. They have been our guiding light.

Love is an intricate dance that can only radiate outward from the physical and emotional fulfillment of the couple. The essential starting point is men's confidence in reciprocating a loving, caring, emotionally and physically fulfilling relationship, when the opportunity is presented.

It is not necessary for everyone to gain the sacred ground of consummating the Yin and Yang physical relationship of love. It is only essential that each individual has the confidence to do so and does not anticipate failure. Confidence in the potential removes the vague uncertainty and unease that permeates every youth's existence. The vague expectation of failure finally humbles the unflagging desire to express love and leaves them with feelings of despair. The mocking disillusionment and parody of love is the end result. At best, a humbled version remains.

The loving perspective can only become characteristic of a race once it becomes embedded within the consciousness that physical love is a real potential for everyone. It is the force that enables the celebration, rather than the disparagement of life. It opens the door to a fulfilling and meaningful life unencumbered by the background noise of the deranged animal that diminishes every effort to be human. Still, though, it is most deeply felt within the physical loving glow of another. It is worth every effort.

The true measure of humanity is how deeply and thoroughly we can love. It is a necessity of self-awareness that cannot be forced. The potential atrophies in men and is brutalized out of women. It can begin to thrive once men become commonly assured of their ability to fulfill the physical act of sex with care.

Men can finally begin to hold their heads high without the false bravado. Women can finally raise their heads without expecting to be brutalized. We can begin to explore and embrace the finer aspects of self-awareness through a loving existence once success in the physical aspects of love becomes common.

Love must become fully understood and accepted in all its nuances before the final curtain will be drawn on the Theater of the Absurd. Love will continue to be a brave endeavor for anyone until it becomes commonly acknowledged and fully understood.

The road to engaging love may initially be difficult, especially for men. Being able to redefine one's nature in a way that radically departs from the existing storyline and millennia of conditioning may take effort. The glow of success helps.

Those that have fully accepted the unimportance of love will cringe at these thoughts of love and lovingly. The beast rationalizes that it is ludicrously counter to being a man. That is *the* gaping hole in our self-awareness. The growing awareness that sexual ineptness causes the farcical 'manly' bravado, self-centeredness, and bombast will encourage men to change soonest. We revolve around that blindspot.

The results of our transcendence begin to boggle the mind. The celebration of love rather than violence is extraordinary to contemplate. If you do not think violence is celebrated, take a look at its preponderance in books, television shows, movies, and video games. Violence is considered entertainment and sex is demoted to a curse. We accept bloody conflict without a second thought while love and its physical component languish.

Acceptance of violence as an endured necessity that cannot be avoided is the fallback position of a failed sentience. The preponderance of violence and hate in our daily lives is staggering, once it is perceived in all its many forms. It is the outlet for the deep-seated feelings of failure as the beast lingers. Isaac Asimov said "violence is the last refuge of the incompetent." He had no idea how thoroughly that phrase defines mankind's current state that we have yet to overcome.

The disparaging, demeaning connotations attached to the terms love and lovingly for men were created in the despair of achieving its physical manifestation. A loving nature that is sensitive and caring is truly manful in that it is human, sentient, and self-aware. The absurd brutish characteristics that are accepted as manly are forced by failure. The attempted taming of men over the millennia has always been a wild goose chase. It has been an attempt to train and tame the monkey. Men engaging in the fulfilling act of making love, rather than bestial lust, transcend the monkey.

Love is not weak, nor is it an effort for the weak. It is a brave, bold effort. The absurdity of men pompously parading their supposed potency and vigour is a confused display of absurdity due to their failure in the physical aspects of love. It is the brute animal preposterously flaunting its failed self-awareness. The monkey reigns and the human is lost while such persists.

The idea of men needing to be harsh and brutal, a blunt instrument, insensitive, small-minded and unemotional is an offense against our self-awareness. The bluster of the worst offenders fills our headlines. The alpha male is a ludicrous portrayal of the monkey. It is so bad, at this point, that sensitive men are often not even considered men at all, even by themselves. When men are too sensitive, they are ludicrously rejected out of hand as unmanly. Sensitivity is manly because it is human. Past attempts to train men to be a 'gentlemanly' monkey was another failed attempt at attaining our humanity.

Two of the worst perceptions that men bear are that their lack of sexual ability is an unusual occurrence that places them in a minority of the male population or, the alternative, that men are all in the muck together and it must be somebody else's fault. Either view further distorts their perceptions of reality thoroughly. The former makes other men their adversary and the latter, their co-conspirators. Women are victims in both cases. Bizarrely, most men seem to carry both thoughts simultaneously.

The broader concepts of a sentient perspective that begin to reveal themselves as men acquire clarity, emotional balance, and self-respect will lead to a completely revamped outlook for mankind. A self-confident, honorable, sensitive sentient perspective can radiate throughout the human race rather than angst, violence, insensitivity, polarization, isolation, and alienation.

Survival

The caring displayed by animals, just as with sex, is an incomplete rendition. A self-aware race changes everything. Our sentience remains distorted as we continue to mimic the monkey and, essentially, remain a beast. It is a broken record that has played for millennia. Our survival depends on something more than the brute, moronic force of an animal. The most intimidating challenges that remain for mankind (including its own lunacy, dystopia, and destructiveness) are not conquered through use of stubborn, moronic, bestial force. That only impedes our progress.

Stabilization is required in order to conquer the subtle challenges presented to our sentience. The forces needed to stabilize mankind emerge with the fulfillment of self-awareness, not blind brutishness. Look around as the beast bashes its way through our existence. We endanger our existence as long as we impersonate the unstable, befuddled beast. A balanced existence between progress, achievement, and fulfillment stabilizes. While a monkey can never grasp that concept, a human can.

The ability to achieve a more balanced existence beyond the beast as well as the necessity to do so are due to our formidable capabilities. We must remove the blinders. Love is not some ephemeral concept of externally applied morality conveyed in sermons. It is an internally generated, self-orienting human concept that liberates the moral compass and goodness within the individual and stabilizes a highly sentient existence. Fulfillment and a moral compass can only be achieved through the internal, self-directed liberation of one's own self-awareness.

A stable outlook on the physical, emotional, and moral planes establishes a race as having fully attained its sentience. It is a rational, stable state for a race that no longer needs to *violently* struggle for survival. Existence will always challenge our sentience, but mindless, bestial violence is counterproductive and destructive for a highly evolved race. We have overcome the bestial challenges that require violence. The inappropriateness of the bestial desire for violence becomes obvious as one notes that it is consistently and insanely directed at mankind itself.

Unhindered self-awareness accepts, fully comprehends, and celebrates the challenges of existence presented to an unobstructed sentient perspective. The complex challenges that our sentient perceptions encounter can only be managed well under such conditions. This does not portray utopia but an awareness of and engagement in a complex existence readily within the purview of our *full* sentient awareness without delusion.

Our intellect and self-awareness sense the disruptive effects caused by the remaining artifacts of our bestial heritage. The continued non-sentient pollution to our view is only due to the blinding inertia of the monkey without intervention, nothing more.

A fine example of the dystopian incongruities within our existence is our befuddled views concerning love and peace. They straddle our animalistic state and our sentient expectations. They are a mainstay of that absurd argument of mankind.

The pompous proposal to fight for love and peace is an obvious attempt to balance animalistic perceptions and sentient awareness. Sentience senses the possibilities. The animal pompously and preposterously justifies lashing out to achieve it. Someone else is always blamed for starting the conflagration.

Whining that love and peace are good, in the expectation that the proclamation itself could change anything, is the other nonsensical alternative. It is the pouting, childish sentient recognition of the destructive residue of our bestial responses. There is no attempt to delve deeper and establish a foundation that eliminates the bestial tendencies. Just pout.

We are simplistic, pragmatic beasts when we fight for love and peace. We are hopeless, helpless dreamers when we loudly clamor for love and peace in the face of destruction and insanity. In absence of unobstructed sentience, the animal will always win out. The hopeless dreamer is ground beneath the boot. The meek inherit nothing in such a scenario. As long as the majority of individuals remain deluded into accepting the monkey, so will mankind, in a dizzying array of delusions.

A sentient perspective incorporates a form of caring that extends far beyond the initial catalyst of physical love. This higher order of caring is first established by overcoming the imbalance in the sexual arrangement of the common animal by expressing care in the act. It results in the sentient, self-aware sophistication of the simplistic form of caring displayed by animals that we call love.

Animals are bad (or, limited, if you rather) at sex. The early adopted assumption was that sex was as unchangeable as the rotation of the Earth. One excuse that developed, in our failure to overcome, was that we dared not intervene. That is only a dodge to justify the inept, despairing, embarrassing inability to overcome the limitations. In the fully human face to face sexual experience the farce is exposed and only one solution remains.

One of the most striking signs that something is terribly wrong is men's inability to easily show affection. It is the beast taking hold and further stunting the already unfulfilled emotions.

There is plenty of evidence that mankind is, at heart, a good, caring, noble race in which the caring is just hindered. Removal of the logjam hampering our sentient perspective will allow our caring nature to flow unimpeded and eliminate the bestial aberrations and destruction. We must become unshackled from the critical, incongruous link to our animal heritage.

Humanity's natural inclination to help others in need is a strong testament to the loving nature of mankind. Love is not a weakness as it is often portrayed today. Love is the strength that mankind must wield to help the race overcome any barrier. The obstacle of non-sentient sex disables it all. We become human when we retain self-respect, self-confidence, discerning determination, emotions, and a loving nature. In other words, our sentient perspective must become undiminished.

Our inability to accept our magnificent state as a sentient being is caused by our certainty that we are nothing more an animal with a big brain. We are so much more than that.

A loving existence (or, a sentient perspective, if that is easier to accept) is the next all-important step in our evolution towards an ordered, highly evolved, sentient existence. The obstruction of our self-awareness impedes. Our high degree of intelligence and hyperawareness, in the absence of this critical metamorphosis, only makes us exceedingly dangerous - and more so every day. Our survival becomes tentative.

A sentient perspective, maintained by caring, fulfilling sex, permits full comprehension of our existence. It is required to direct and command our highly evolved, complex endeavors. It enhances our ability to survive and overcome the complex challenges encountered by our heightened awareness. We must turn our attention away from the delusions of the beast that have mesmerized us and focus our attention on the sentient challenges. The human sentient perspective must flourish.

Threads of the tapestry

As one begins to grasp the essentials of what is being portrayed in these writings, it becomes straightforward to understand how the two genders influenced all of history. The effect of those two threads of the tapestry are all that count.

The female gender has, subtly and gently, nudged us in the right direction. Their gentle, subtle, sentient insistence has been our saving grace. It has continually attempted to right the ship. Their relatively intact sentience has always striven to limit the bloodshed. The most obvious example is the slow non-violent way in which they have attempted to overcome sexism.

Unfortunately, women could never understand or resolve that which disturbs men. They could only attempt to tame the beast which could never right the ship completely.

Men endured the terrible feeling of failure and attempted to hide from it down through the ages. The desire to deceive, the bluster, the combative stance and self-interest were facilitated by the circumstances. Men engaged in the disastrous pastime of seeking scapegoats that began with women. Childish finger pointing became a mainstay of our existence, even to the level of nations. Even though not always fully implemented by each individual, the distortions to the perceptions of the male gender wreak havoc on our sentience as the beast remains. We have always accepted the beast without acknowledging the fact.

The conditioned mass consensus regarding the delusion at the foundation of our existence reinforces the conclusion that we cannot change. We erroneous accept an animal's existence, never fully realizing that the human is far more than just the smart, lying, disturbed, deluded animal it pretends to be.

We can change our existence once we look in the mirror and use our intellect to change our circumstances. In the meantime, the beast fiddles with trifling issues and creates more delusions. The isolating bestial state flourishes, and mankind burns. The beast requires removal, not training for its antics.

Our hyperawareness more emphatically senses the disparity of the situation as time progresses. Our sentience and inherent honesty rebel at the lie pervading our existence. Further devastation to our sentience occurs as the truth is unsuccessfully sought and the threads of Yin and Yang never fully entwine.

Achievement

Mankind has been blessed with the potential for a sentient perspective. We tantalizingly and disturbingly sense and impatiently await its realization. The slow process of taming the beast is not the way forward for a self-aware race. We are not beasts. The immediacy of attaining a sentient perspective is utterly lost in the confusion of the beast. Emergence from the bestial state does not need to take further millennia.

Without physical love, we delude ourselves into believing everything is slowly getting better, until it all comes crashing down around our heads, once again. Exit from this Theater of the Absurd and the beast is immediate, once begun in earnest.

We hide from our sexual nature in shame and delay our fulfillment. This essential necessity of life is seldom mentioned at all, in any context. We avoid its mention with every effort. In light of the importance of sex to our existence, it is ludicrous that we sulk, skulk and desperately avoid the subject, even within one's own mind. The bestial state of sex disturbs everything.

Men's strong desire for sex ensures that defeating, self-serving, bestial behaviour continues in the absence of the act of physical love. Subconscious awareness is ever-present, even if it is never articulated. It creates conflict with compassion and our sentient awareness. Selfish bestial desires and the delusions to our self-awareness displace a sentient perspective.

Our heightened awareness of the situation remains whether we like it or not. Rebellion against the shame of lust is no better than the shame itself. The only resolution is distinguishing between human love-making and bestial rutting. A sentient gains his self-awareness by accepting that the latter is obsolete in man.

Our hyperawareness is meant to interpret a more comprehensive sense of reality. It is not meant to distort reality through deceptions bred to explain away or ignore any significant failure that our self-awareness makes apparent. As long as our perceptions remain distorted, we compromise our existence and fall well short of a sentient perspective. In the ongoing clamour of our sexual failure, we accept the beast.

Our sentience rebels against the rationalizations that are required by a sentient being of either gender engaging in unfulfilling sex. Experiencing reciprocal physical satisfaction and the emotional outlet of caring is essential for both. We know that there is something missing and only accept it as unchangeable in our despair. That sets the failure of mankind in motion in both genders. A human that ruts remains an animal. It belittles and confounds the magnificence of our humanity.

The nonsensical precept that mankind is broken and sentience is a curse remands us into misery. It commits us to our ongoing failure and dystopia. We justify acting like an animal and dangerously abandon our sentience. We embrace 'the animal spirit'. 'Everyone for themselves' is an animal's suggestion.

We are never so hopeless as when we consider humanity. Dystopia is considered the deserved result of our sentience. We endure the monkey rather than revel in the human. 'Too bad that some must suffer so much. Glad it ain't me!'

Imagine growing up in a setting surrounded by humans fully engaged and confident in life, filled with compassion rather than ineptness, arrogance, insensitivity, delusion, and indifference.

Relying on some accepted, predetermined set of behaviour for the monkey and enforcing any transgressions is a bestial adaptation. It encourages dystopia and adds to the delusion that we are actually improving while the mental state of humanity continues to deteriorate so slowly that we don't notice.

Sentient Survival

A sentient perspective is a survival mechanism for an animal that is so intelligent that it could wipe itself off the map as awareness, perceptions, and knowledge otherwise grow in moronic fashion. Restraint, reason, and balance become imperative. A balanced sentient perspective provides a moral compass and context for sentience. It cannot be attained through unsubstantiated, forced moral strictures or legislation.

A sentient perspective is the long term survival mechanism for a sentient race. Its absence does not lead to immediate extinction, but without its guidance, sentient existence becomes more and more troublesome, disruptive, and dystopian.

Care fulfilling the act of sex makes self-aware existence meaningful, beyond the mindless urges of the beast. The race's sentient perspective begins to flourish when sexual fulfillment becomes commonplace. This riddle becomes more pressing as our awareness develops further. Acceptance of the failure of the bestial rendition of sex is not a viable option as a sentient race advances. Our survival becomes tentative.

War is the current alternative to sanity. We ruthlessly wipe each other off the map. Like that's going to help. The aftermath of war used to sober us for a while as we realized the devastation that our animal outbursts caused. That has begun to fade, even as science advances the weaponry. The moronic, blinded beast shrugs its shoulders. 'What's to be done?', it says.

Inventiveness and creativity need to be channeled through a sentient perspective rather than deceived by a corrupted will bent to self-destruction. A fully self-aware sentient perspective is the survival mechanism of a race that becomes so sophisticated it can eventually cause vast destruction or creation.

We relinquish our sentient perspective and flirt with destruction as long as we remain a beast. The beast blinds itself to the lack that sentient awareness cannot avoid acknowledging and pursues its own destruction. The solution is now provided. The awareness, will, and discipline to enact it are now required. Humanity must bring its intellect to bear in order to overcome.

The fulcrum

Sex is a tiny fulcrum that currently misdirects our sentient perspective thoroughly. It overturns our sanity and reason.

We languish in an untenable state between beast and sentience because of the seemingly insurmountable problem that lurks in our existence. We have not reached our potential, not even close. The juggernaut of bestial sex remains to debilitate us.

Sex becomes more and more perverted in a self-aware race in the absence of consummating it in a caring manner. Obsessions are enforced by men's driving desire for sex *in tandem* with the repetitive lack of fulfillment. The urge to sex is not the problem. Non-sentient enactment is.

Making love is just a small, but essential, component of human, sentient life. Once the fulfilling nature of the self-aware sexual model becomes common, sex will no longer remain an obsession. It will be complete and fulfilling and acted on as such. We can move on to explore fulfillment of a sentient existence as we put away the all-consuming, obsessive behaviours of failure.

It must not be misconstrued that the physical expression of love is the fulfilling end result. It is not the goal. It is a necessary milestone on the way to a sentient perspective. It is the leverage that lifts us into a fulfilling life and clear perspective. It clarifies that humanity is much, much more than just an animal.

Mankind is an animal that consciously perceives the discrepancies in sex as the beast continues to enact it. There is no avoiding it. We cannot abandon our self-awareness. Who would want to? The loving, fulfilling sexual model makes existence whole for humanity, eliminating the common perversions and obsessions that our skewed sentient view develops to fill the gap.

Celebration and fulfillment, rather than disappointment and indignity, become the order of the day when physical, emotionally fulfilled love is achieved.

The flow

It seems unreasonable that the way we perform a single, seemingly simple, activity can transform our existence. Yet, that is what all of the evidence supports. It continues to drag us back to our animal origins. Sex is a tremendously important aspect of existence. It cannot be avoided. Until it reaches its sentient potential, we dupe ourselves into remaining a beast rather than do without.

Our self-awareness revealed the profound concept that sex can be more than an act of one-sided self-gratification. We know it in the depths of our consciousness. We become flummoxed by the realization without the fulfillment. In its fulfillment, the sentient perspective is released and relieved. Satisfaction and emotional fulfillment must be achieved for both.

We have slowly been gaining insights to shred the conditioning and stupor that arrested our development. We remain little different from the cowering animal emerging from its cave until we put this final piece in place. We picked up many pieces of understanding along the way, but never put all of the pieces together. As we makes this final leap, we become human.

Freud is a perfect example of the way in which our scope has been constrained and the mainstay of our existence has remained obsessive. It *has* been all about sex. From the limited perspective of the beast, he was right and amazingly insightful. He just didn't realize it need not be just about sex nor the reason that it remained so. He concluded that sex itself was the problem and we just had to deal with the obsessions. Our obsessions with sex are only due to its colossal sentient failure, not its' very existence. We obsess due to the sentient failure of sex.

Once fulfilled, it will no longer be just about sex. It will be about life. This final step opens us to a reasoning existence in which we can face the universe with confidence and overcome the baffled delusions of the beast. It permits the self-aware being to look in the mirror with acceptance rather than horror.

A sentient perspective develops with acceptance of self and, thereby, retention of self-respect. It is a substantive state that is retained or abdicated. It is a state of our existence that must become common. We tried preaching that we should be good. When that didn't work, we decided to try legal systems and punishment which also is an utter failure. Let's try something that really can work. Let's liberate our souls.

Transcendentalism and the Flower Power movement both come astonishingly close to comprehending our sentient dilemma from two entirely different perspectives. They both stumbled within view of the final, adequate sentient perspective required to overcome our dilemma. Previous efforts and insights had already begun to orient the human closer and closer to the truth.

Transcendentalism was driven by a sense that mankind's goodness and loving ability are inherent and undermined. The Flower Power movement was driven by the sense that sex was compromised and love was downtrodden. They both hint at mankind's potential magnificence. Both are profoundly insightful while lacking the finishing touches that converge in sentience.

Transcendentalism insightfully proposes that the goodness of mankind is inherent but forcibly purged. It just did not suggest a viable way to retain our goodness. The Flower Power movement insightfully proposes that sex and love are both good and realizes their importance. It just did not equate the two.

We claim our goodness through the liberation of the act of making love. Fulfilling sex liberates our goodness and love. Goodness, a caring nature, and loving sex critically and intricately entwine to fulfill a loving, sentient perspective.

Life's advancement of awareness is inexorable. Evolution leads to heightened awareness. Increasing awareness is an improvement in life. Loving sex is a crucial measure of awareness for a self-aware race that proclaims their arrival at a sentient perspective and state of existence.

The evolution of awareness

Self-awareness can be described as the articulation of existence in context to oneself. The eye to eye sexual encounter initiated a disturbing awareness regarding the awful lack in the sexual experience that we have desperately avoided articulating. This resulted in enforcement of delusion. That delusion continually expands to justify the original deception.

One of the first casualties was the sad result that women became inappropriately suppressed. We never even admit the obvious conclusion that the male gender, not just a few individuals, cause misogyny and sexism. It just happened. Right.

What could possibly cause a sentient race to delude itself so thoroughly? What could possibly deform us to the extent that we accept the state of sexism on a global scale? We blindly accept the premise that women are abused and disdained and just try to train the monkey not to act it out. That is insane.

Taming, shaming or training the male gender into good behaviour does not resolve the problem. One can sympathize with the woman's plight, but real resolution is only provided by the male gender accepting their responsibility for fulfilling sex.

A few men gaining the ability to satisfy only distorts further. It is deemed a personal conquest rather than the expected outcome within the confines of our current state of delusion and selfish, bestial context of existence.

Our hyperawareness continually gains momentum and achieves new insights into our existence. These new insights are rationalized as necessary to align with previous deceptions. We become more haunted by the deceits as we accept these more confoundingly blatant deceptions. Deceit becomes more accepted as reasoning becomes more compromised. It is an expanding bubble of insanity as we further indulge the beast.

The continued fraying of our existence makes some people long for the past in which we deluded ourselves with moral strictures that have no sound basis beyond the limited sense that we should be good. These views from the past were an inept substitute for the more substantive internal moral compass that is required. Pining for the 'good old days' that never were is a sham.

As the obvious holes became punched in the trance of baseless moral strictures babbled by self-appointed paragons of virtue, more hopeless mindsets became the new mainstay. We stray even closer to the beast. These 'liberated views' pervasively depict the more dangerous view that morality is meaningless. The 'animal spirit' is more fully accepted. Either view deludes and undermines humanity's potential. Responsibility for our existence is avoided and the beast still rules.

For the individual, the situation is bafflingly opaque due to the preconditioning and the evolving nature of life. In the early days of puberty, sex is relished as something wonderful. One begins to buckle under preprogrammed acceptance of despair as the incomplete act of sex becomes appallingly apparent. The devolution of awareness begins in the desperate cover-up.

The deficient situation consumes life as it progresses. Self-awareness is sacrificed in the desperate desire to contend with the gaping hole in life. The individual becomes mired in a stupor while retaining a dangerously unchecked intellect that increasingly unleashes its frustration and fury on existence or retreats into self-destructive despair.

In youth, before complete surrender, peaks of awareness often pierce the veils of distortion to suggest that there should be something more. Uncorrupted youthful intuition suggests something is wrong, but full articulation is impeded by conditioning. We come closer each time to breaking the veil.

The Flower Power movement was just such a desperate, blind, instinctual search that one generation attempted. The attempt to break free from our insanity was assisted by the slow, ongoing background accrual of knowledge over the ages. "*Free* love", of course, was just another blind alley but came so very close to the answer that it is painful to contemplate. It proclaimed what our sentience has been screaming all along. Sex is important! Love is important! Once again, it failed though, by substituting lots of 'free' sex, in the form of lust, for love-making.

'Free Love' allowed men and women to engage in sex more often, but without the satisfaction and fulfillment required. The unbridled lust, termed 'Free Love', proved to be nothing more than a repackaging of men's desperate desire for sex without awareness or acceptance of responsibility. Fulfillment remained missing. We have always been stumbling closer to the profound truth. Finally, we must proclaim that the *physical* aspects of love, in the form of sex, are *essential* to love. *That* is the breakthrough.

Nature's way

The final culmination of humanity's millennia-long marathon to complete the maturation process has always been ready for us. Nature prepared for the eventuality in so many ways that it is remarkable. Engaging in sex while gazing in each other's eyes was one of those preparations. It seems an intentional nudge for our self-awareness in the direction of the final fulfillment of the act of sex called love-making. It could not be ignored forever (Nature: Hint! Hint! Mankind: Huh?). Face to face sex makes it clear that something is missing each time we thrust into the face of failure. It is prescient of the necessary end result.

Our growing awareness has also prepared us for the eventual sentient perspective in another direction. Animals are true to their nature. We have not been. Since we developed those early myths, our growing consciousness has sensed that something was playing us false. On two fronts, sex and our inherent honesty, we have always known something was wrong. We could not seem to conquer the first, so we befuddled the second. We just needed to unashamedly admit that animal sex is not enough for a human and, then, overcome that hurdle without assistance from labs, factories, or other appendages. The responsibility lies wholly with the obdurate, excuse-laden man to overcome the lack. There are many more such hints provided.

Most importantly, nature provides for an intellect to puzzle out the resolution to men's difficulty. The elegance of nature's preparedness for sentience is truly remarkable. Lasting long enough is the final, necessary requirement. It opens the final door through which men can begin to explore full measures of making love and being human.

Now, we can complete the sentient picture. It makes one appreciate the elegance and grace of nature.

It also makes one wonder whether all of the preparatory steps that nature took to improve sex were actually the critical initial impetus towards becoming sentient. Chicken and egg.

We can now head towards the exit of the Theater of the Absurd in an orderly manner. Tragedies, farcical comedies, and high drama may have seen their final days.

For an interesting eye opener, look up tragedy ("goat song") and its historical connection to the Dionysian cults.

Metamorphosis

We bring evolution to a higher order by enacting the art of making love. This brings us beyond genetic evolution. We consciously, not genetically, transcend the animal state.

The fulfillment unleashes and brings to bear every aspect of our sentient perspective including awareness, discipline, will, creativity, compassion, thought, and knowledge without distraction. We attain balance. It is as if we have only been half-alive, half-human, and far too close to the beast. Only our intellect has flourished, while our self-awareness, which can only be fulfilled in honesty, reason, and goodness, has been absent.

It is like a shuttered light that should shine out from the heart in two directions. The internally-directed light of self-respect illuminates and banishes the darkness in the corners of our minds. The light that shines out reveals we have constructed all of the nightmares of our existence. As we look at others, we can begin to perceive the human rather than the beast.

This radical transformation in our perspective concerning reality is tremendously significant. Unstable, witless, disturbed animalistic adolescence transforms into a mature, considered, human self-confidence. It finally removes us from the subhuman state of the intelligent, violent, dangerous beast that makes our existence a grubbing betrayal of our sentience.

The dystopia we endure is nothing more than a distracted, aggravated adolescence in which we have been caught between bestial instincts and sentient insights. We have groped to understand a subject that appears simple, but contains perplexing shortcomings in its primitive form, and has vast implications for a race that is aware of its own existence.

Our progress has been constrained to blind, selfish, materialistic, bestial endeavors at the expense of the human, sentient spirit. The beast has ruled our existence and the light of a loving, sentient perspective has been dimmed to the point of nearly being extinguished. It is time for the human spirit to rule unfettered in a universe of vast potential.

Existing in the context of mutual benefit becomes a necessity for a race with the potential for mass destruction at its fingertips. It is crucial and *much* more suited for a sentient race's complex, sophisticated interactions.

Split Infinity

Infinity splits into the rabid beast of the past and the humans that will populate the future as we begin our metamorphosis into a sentient creature and spread our wings. It is based on our acceptance and understanding of the importance of physical love that can finally flourishes.

Our consciousness begins to fill with wonder in the aftermath of contemplating a fulfilled sexual experience. Reason and emotional balance begin to occupy the human perspective. A moral compass begins to develop. The human emerges. Sexism, misogyny, domestic violence, duplicity, and a host of other nonsense can quickly wither to nothing.

The wonder of love originates in sex, where it has hidden for ages. Love is a word that has meaning. It is the sentient expression of caring that transcends the beast. It is the fulfillment of the sentient state. Lust, *in a sentient race*, perverts and destroys the potential. Loving sex inaugurates the wonder of a sentient experience.

The broader aspects of a sentient perspective can become realized once a race becomes sophisticated enough to incorporate reciprocal care into the act of sex and, thus, retain its self-respect and unobscured perceptions.

Our intelligence allows us to resolve the crucial sexual conundrum exposed by our sentient self-awareness to, thus, move beyond the mindless rutting of lesser animals. A sentient perspective is the expansive result as we transcends the brute mentality and split infinity. Permanently and decisively we become something far more than just an animal.

All of the aspects of love are so suited to a fully sentient existence as to astonish. Its distortions underpin our dystopia. The liberation of mankind is dependent on the vast potential of love. Our sophistication is lost when sex is relegated to the limited act of rutting like an animal. It is impossible to ponder love in the aftermath of enduring the offensive, mindless, negligent, apathetic, excuse-laden, bestial rutting.

We can only truly distinguish ourselves from animals through the transcendent physical act of loving that opens the door for mankind to love thoroughly. We only become human, a magnificent creature, as we leave the beast completely behind.

Nobility

Our emotional disorientation can only be overcome by developing our ability to make love. Emotional suppression and confusion is due to the inability to articulate love and the ongoing abdication of our self-awareness. We must learn to care at a level far transcending the common animal. The props used throughout history to mimic confidence and nobility are nothing more than the beast mimicking self-awareness. It becomes a game of delusion.

The compassion and outpouring of care whenever there is some form of disaster is just the slightest expression of the potential goodness and nobility that resides within humanity. It only needs to find release from the absurd contradictions and distractions inherent in the remnants of the beast. Goodness is part of the evolving nature of a noble existence.

Reason tried to break out about three thousand years ago but became mystified and confused amidst the sexual dilemma. The full aspects of the sentient perspective remain to be articulated as we begin to experience the widespread physical aspects of love within the race. Self-awareness underpins it all.

Emotions radiate outward through our interactions with others. The home represents the smallest subset of society. It is where both the disruption and the resolution of our existence begin. Frustration, angst, negativity, distrust, paranoia, deceit, and violence are the common type of emotions that radiate outward from the home today into all of the interactions of the human race. It is masked in the disguise of courtesy that was developed to avoid getting brained by another animal. Nowadays, we call it political correctness, which is the best the beast can do.

Unforced confidence, compassion, acceptance, honesty, and inclusion can begin to radiate outward from the home. This may sound wide-eyed, naive, and innocent. It is so much more hard-nosed than you can possibly imagine. It is real. Lust is for brutes, making love is for humans. I would say angels but that would just confuse some.

The physical expression of love will remove an obstruction that instigates and maintains a great deal of the turbulence surrounding mankind's existence. It is a real change, finally, not just another coat of whitewash on our dystopia.

The barriers that we hide behind isolate us. They begin to collapse as we attain our self-assured nature. As we look in the mirror we can finally find ourselves more than acceptable.

We can become fully human, a noble creature. There are no inherent nightmares, monsters, demons, evil, or necessary battles to be fought between members of a fully sentient race. The nightmares and delusions that have haunted us from our distant past will take some time to give way to a noble perspective. You should be able to taste it by now, though.

The end result for mankind is a courteous, gentle, well-mannered, well-intentioned approach to life that is forged in steel, accepts no excuses, abides no delusions, and progresses with rationality. That future is enabling, acceptant, fulfilling, loving, noble, and truly profound. We can fully embrace our existence and face the complex challenges presented to our sentience with confidence, reason, and compassion.

Progressions

Surrounded by the debris of our failed attempts to achieve sentience, mired in the detritus of deceit and confusion, we have exacerbated our own misery. We continually raise the noise level of our delusions to drown out the ever-increasing clamour of our growing awareness that something is fundamentally wrong.

The progression of conditioning and dystopia that we have endured has been matched by an adamant refusal to accept that this is all we are. We have continuously hammered against the closed door of our stupor.

The bewildering impetus to confusion has been matched by a desperate sentient search for the flaw in our existence. We first emerged from the caves while reinforcing the darkness in an utter, blinding confusion that continued grow. In tandem, we slowly began to sense the boundaries of the problem. Yin and Yang went to work in conflicting directions.

The painful assault on our sentience and reason became increasingly burdensome as our perceptions progressed. The blinders remained in the midst of blatant incongruity and delusion. The blinders are gone. Now, we can finally break through the confusion impeding our understanding to identify the source and its resolution. Yin and Yang can now align.

Neither sex nor sentience is a curse, but a challenge to refine. Sex must be rectified to even begin. It is easy to do once acknowledged. All of the misleading methods currently in vogue regarding the subject of sex (e.g. the little blue pill, alternative means, pursuits, and mechanical assists) are just craven attempts and sleight of hand to avoid confronting the issue directly. That was doomed from the start. It could never work.

The final growing realization that women deserve sexual satisfaction is profound. It finally unlocked the door. All we need now do is walk through it. Mankind can only fully overcome the problems presented by engaging eye to eye in a loving tangle. No assist to the sexual engagement, other than the care, intellect, and discipline, can fully liberate the sentient perspective and a fulfilling existence. It has to be a fully human endeavor.

The shortcomings of lust are only acceptable to the stupor of an animal. Fulfillment of loving, eye to eye, makes us human.

The Individual

What happens to the human condition if the vast majority of humanity retains its self-respect? What if reason, rather than blindly arguing admittedly foolish positions ("the lesser of two evils" is an admission of foolishness) presides? No more 'us and them' is one result.

If one is driven by self-respect and successfully defends one's own integrity, everything changes radically. Many of the current systems and structures of mankind may stabilize without significant change to their contexts. For those of you still entrenched in the conditioning, this will seem a preposterous suggestion. What's the point of indulging a fairy tale, right? Mankind getting along with each other seems ludicrous in the current combative, vicious, paranoid setting. Once the individual is freed from delusion, anything is possible, even thinking.

Full emergence from the imperfect sentient state in which we currently exist is the next stage of our evolution. It is evolution of the individual into a state in which consciousness and self-awareness finally become cherished. In some ways, it is evolution into goodness, or evolution into a more natural state of a fully expressed sentient, self-aware existence in which goodness is part of the natural order. We become true to our sentient state.

Final resolution

All of the revolutions that litter our history have little to do with any real change and everything to do with lashing out at the clamoring pain, confusion, and delusion regarding our deficient state.   Revolution has never had much of an effect because it never addressed the source of our issues, the individual.   It only fortified the rabid distortions.

Sentient sex is a grass roots change at the level of the individual.   It is an evolution of consciousness.   It begins with the realization that rutting is for animals and ends in love-making and responsible, self-aware humans.   This change knows no borders, needs no leaders, and can spread like wildfire.   It is led by each individual liberating themselves.   It is supported by the desperate self-aware desire of men to satisfy their lovers.   It is individuals picking up the pieces of their sentience and moving on.   It is the natural transition of mankind into a more complete, unimpeded state of sentient existence.

A balanced existence

The universe will finally face a sentient race with full possession of its faculties as it moves forward with reason, balance, and an underlying exuberance.   Self-respect, emotional stability, and reason can finally become the cornerstones that give our existence stability.

Our delusional *perceived* progress in the material realm can be replaced with *actual* progress that is more balanced, thoughtful, and beneficial.   Emotional instability and the desire for personal gain at any cost currently dominate the decision-making processes that reflect the economic theory of a monkey.   Honour and integrity make different decisions.   Self-respect, self-confidence, and empathy preside over a different existence.

An explosion of beneficial endeavors that are personally fulfilling can begin to permeate our existence as mankind learns to trust itself.   We can create real improvements in our state.

The spiritual, moral, and ethical aspects of our existence have been trampled more than ever in our stupor over the last century (reminds me of my favorite song by Enya).   It is time for vast improvements.   None will be able to resist the urge to sing.

The wings of sentience

Fear and its accompanying desire for security and protection will dwindle. The primary desire for protection today is from one's fellow man. How absurd is that? Distrust rules.

It is time to spread our sentient wings and fly. Integrity grounded in self-respect will provide for different decisions throughout our lives. Our spirit can finally soar. Ponder a world in which each person looks into the eyes of another that mirrors their own full confidence in life and each other. That is the point at which a sentient perspective begins to take a fierce hold on our existence and never lets go. We will learn what it really means to fly. Mankind will finally shed its inhumanity and feelings of isolation. We can begin to discover our humanity.

We will begin to sense the exuberance. The changing sense of what is important will slowly liberate mankind from the absurdity of our current situation in which distrust, vileness, and insanity rule.

On the surface, nothing of import will herald the change. All of the typical day-to-day activities will continue. It is the undertone and texture of the interaction that will begin to portend the tremendous tsunami of change.

A loving relationship

How much will the landscape of love for one other person above all others change? It seems likely that this particular endeavor will change most of all. After all, it is at center stage of the Theater of the Absurd. Misogyny and sexism lie in closest proximity to the heart of the absurdity that distorts and fouls every aspect of our lives.

Due to men's inferiority complex, preposterous and appalling games are sadly played out by both genders to determine who is 'lovable'. In this bizarre situation, the woman is subjugated in order to compensate for the man's failure. The whole process has been perfected in colossal perversion. Every aspect surrounding the personal relationship will need to be re-examined thoroughly.

Our brute approach to life is never more apparent than in all stages of the mating dance. The submissiveness of women is a highly desired quality by many men. Even when not directly desired, it still underlies all of the interactions between the two sexes and the development of our societies. This offensive subjugation of women is the lead-in to misogyny, sexism, and all forms of obsession and perversion.

Men's fear of sexual failure clouds every aspect of romantic entanglement and our lives, from initiation to conclusion. Insecurities of each gender make the whole exercise ludicrous.

The seeming insecurities of women are due to the unacknowledged efforts of men to instill that insecurity. Physical and verbal domestic violence and sexual abuse are just two of the most blatant instances. The subterfuge lies deep beneath every interaction of the two genders throughout our lifetimes. Many interactions are played out in the fumbling, bestial game of dominance. Altogether, it has been an absurd few thousand years that is getting rapidly worse. It is finally time to turn it around.

Women will finally be able to display their womanliness and femininity rather than flaunt their sexuality or hide behind the many masks purposely donned to avoid the crude obsessions of men. Men will no longer be bound into the stupor of a brutish, animal-like caricature. All, not just intimate, relationships will be redefined radically in new terms based on self-respect.

What happens when a person learns to love themselves without reservation? If you truly love all of life without reservation, will finding someone? with whom to spend a lifetime? become nearly effortless? We will just have to wait and see how it unfolds.

Sanity

The closest we have come to sanity in the past is after widespread conflagration and devastation. That is not sanity. It is the sobering, temporary awareness of how vicious and unruly our bestial existence can become. For a little while, the inherent graceful qualities of mankind tentatively appear. Then, once again, our broken sentience asserts itself and we plunge into bestial nonsense and outright viciousness, once again.

The repetitive cycle of vast destruction followed by limited, temporary bubbles of civility, ad nauseam, define our past. The vague, tentative sense of hope, courtesy, civility, and imagination always gives way to the loud clamorings of the beast in the depths of its pompous stupor, arrogance, and idiocy. The offensive, brute caricature becomes celebrated as bold behaviour by the most idiotic simpletons. We proceed over the cliff, reach a peak of self-destruction, and start all over again. Do you see that perilous cliff? We are peering over the precipice as this is written.

We have become so convinced that this is our natural state that the threat of mutual destruction is accepted (punishment, once again). We endorse the idea of reciprocal nuclear destruction as the most bizarre means of 'keeping the peace' and, ridiculously, only fear the *further* proliferation of nuclear weapons to other nations!

This ultimate example of our paranoia and applying the threat of punishment to Pavlov's dog on a global scale proves our current insanity and convictions regarding our absurdity beyond a doubt. The beast now rules in a very dangerous situation.

Our memory of the pain and insanity of upheaval never lasts as long as a single generation's lifespan. Even if our destructive capabilities were to set us back thousands of years without utterly obliterating our existence, still we would not face the fact of our insane destructive tendencies. This is the typical sci-fi scenario that accepts our derangement as all others do. The most speculative of writers can't see past the beast.

The generation born into relative peace (in other words, all destruction is at a distance) just reads about destruction as if it were another fascinating, unimportant fiction. They are not branded with the painful awareness of the consequences of the worst that our paranoid existence can wreak. Literally, out of sight, out of (our) mind(s). Bombs are not falling around their heads, therefore we have improved or it is just a minor problem to ignore until the bombs hit home. Those that have retained some empathy and honesty, hopelessly and helplessly watch as the upheaval increases, once again. The righteous and utterly arrogant willfully accept that destruction rather than see their own senseless delusions or alleged pompous importance overturned.

The sanity of a sentient, self-aware creature does not rely on fear or threat of destruction. Those are the considerations of a beast still cowering in its cave. The race's dangerously violent, confused, and deluded adolescence must become something only read in history books. Sanity is based on an undistorted view of reality that is intimately and unashamedly aware of the magnificence that mankind can attain and an undistracted focus on its attainment.

Sapience

This book states that love is something inherent in a mature sentient model that is only fulfilled by loving sex. That an unobscured sentient perspective provided by retained self-respect is an integral, crucial part of an honest, self-aware existence.

A sentient perspective, though, is not the end of the line. It is only the basis for a sane existence. Sanity is just the beginning. Our sapience, or wisdom, is the next step that can only flourish with the unleashing of emotional balance and reason. A sentient perspective is essential to achieving sapience.

No better labels than animal lust and stupor describe our current despairing antics, not just our sexual expression. The connotations of the words suit all of the rampant aspects of our situation. It continues to define us as a rabid, confused and self-deluding creature in an ongoing struggle between sentient awareness and bestial expression. The lust for life is no more than the bestial, corrupted remnant of the undistorted expression of love that is consonant with a sentient existence. Only unobstructed self-awareness can differentiate us from the beast.

A sentient perspective begins with the accepted potential for a cherishing, intimate relationship between two people which expands to encompass all human interactions and relationships. It governs a human, sentient, sane state of existence. It establishes and reinforces self-respect. The potential for a cherishing shared existence between two people abolishes the absurd behaviour of the subhuman and fortifies the finer qualities of mankind that are concurrent with a sentient perspective.

Empathy and tempered innocence are currently numbed out of the cultural imperative for humanity. They are burdened, compromised and abused into oblivion. Empathy may be the most profound result of fulfilled sentience that leads to sapience.

Sanity and a sentient perspective are not just the temporary good manners created in the horrified aftermath of mass destruction. Survival of empathy at the individual level and displacement of the inferiority-ridden ego with self-respect, changes mankind permanently. It is not just the intermittent throes of good behaviour that delude us into believing all is getting better, while simultaneously preparing for the next, more destructive assault on our existence.

Innocence restored

Call it innocent eyes, if you like. Tempered innocence is part of a sentient perspective. It is the knowledgeable, insightful innocence that is currently twisted out of existence by the deceit and subterfuge endured.

Innocence is portrayed as a weakness that is abandoned as one reaches the brute 'maturity' of stupor that relinquishes innocence to delusions of despair that obscure self-awareness.

Innocent inclinations must become acknowledged as appropriate and fulfilling, not a fanciful dream of the weak-minded. The mindless brute revels in 'maturity'.

Tempered innocence is forged in the fire of a fully sentient perspective and existence. Tempered innocence and sapience have strong ties that have always been recognized.

Innocence takes a great deal of courage at this point in time. Courageous innocence has been displayed by the best of women and the rarest of men throughout the race's disturbed adolescence.

The untapped potential

One of the most fascinating considerations is that change will go so far beyond our current limited, distorted perspective that it becomes difficult to fully describe. The roots of this further potential, though, can be traced to relief from the effects of mankind's current desire to bury its head in the sand of nonsense.

Mankind blinds itself in the impractical desire to avoid facing the self-delusion regarding the animal sexual model. The end effect of this forced conditioning is the inability to think clearly.

Within this unstable state, change becomes a drastic, fearful thing. Thought is, thus, constrained to an extent that hobbles the senses.

We tend not to trust change or deep thought. In our state of delusion and deceit, distrust of anything new is common due to the inbred fear that any thinking might stumble on that which we are unwilling to face. Bluster, self-interest, stupor, and consensus are what remains. A confident, emotionally stable, sentient race would trust its nature and accept its ability to think clearly.

This does not forebode quick change but bold, sapient, substantive change created by a race that finally, really thinks.

Codifying a sentient existence

The great conversation regarding mankind's existence and place in the world can finally proceed beyond the endless, foolish argument that bickers to no avail and no real answers. The grand preposterous argument filled with ludicrously polarized, contentious positions squabbling to justify selfishly distorted, delusional, paranoid perspectives that are born in self-deception, self-interest, and self-hate can fade. The inappropriate burdens of mankind, driven by the delusion-induced bizarrely aberrant views of the individual, can end. Uninhibited, unfettered self-awareness changes everything.

All of the foibles we endure are indicative of a broken self-awareness. A sentient creature that fully transcends the state of the monkey recognizes its own magnificence and no longer hides.

The absurdities and insanities that pollute our existence can dissipate. Our desperate need for purposeless, distracting stimulation can dwindle. A sentient being's fulfilling existence need not indulge in mindless fascination with inconsequentials and distraction through observing the antics of fools in the headlines. A loving, accepting existence ensures stimulation of the thought processes and a life of honest, fulfilling effort rather than abortive attempts to express oneself without any effort.

The massive drag of deception that leaves our intelligence in tact but destroys our self-awareness, innocence, empathy, emotional balance, and reason, convincing us that we are faulty by design, can end. The vast difference between our nature and our faulty condition will finally become appallingly apparent. Thorough clarification and classification of the human condition can finally occur.

The re-codification will be seen in our actions as the sentient perspective of humanity orients itself. The true form of our nature will become apparent as the fog of ancient babble dissipates. Our actions will depict self-awareness, sentience, and love. Mankind will learn that it is not a disturbed monkey, but a self-aware creature with only the weakest ties to its predecessors.

We are a race that can be consistent with its sentient nature. We can finally exist as a stunningly fully formed work of art. A sentient existence has nothing of which to be ashamed. We can finally gaze in the mirror with wonder rather than horror.

Dystopia banished

This is not some wide-eyed belief in utopia or perfection. Challenges, of course, will continue to exist, at the level of individual and couples right on up through mankind's existence itself. But, the challenge presented by self-induced dystopia can vanish into the void where it belongs. The real challenges to our existence can only be overcome by undiluted, stable, sentience equipped with reason, thought, balance, and confidence.

We won't lie around in fields of lotus flowers letting life drift away. *That* is more descriptive of the current blind, hopeless desire of the beast to escape from the absurdity of its dystopian existence. We will be more engaged in life than ever because the experience will be fulfilling, not just the toleration of misery.

We never even question the existence of our dystopia or its cause because of the ingrained conditioning. Useless, blinded, mindless, bombastic avoidance is the mainstay of our stupor. Mesmerized by our ongoing superficial failures and blind to our fundamental failure, we accept dystopia and remain bestial.

Breaking the chain

Mankind has been held back by a single, imperceptible chain that stretches all the way back beyond the first glimmering of sentience to nature's initial implementation of sexual reproduction. The links in the chain that enthrall mankind are the myths, paradigms, deceits, obsessions, and perversions that we continue to develop while avoiding truth. They obscure the reality that sex can be something more for a fully sentient race. It is time to break the chain to pieces and rise from our groveling, furtive, paranoid, near-fetal, bestial position and attain our sentience.

The inherent qualities of a fully self-aware existence are self-confidence, honor, integrity, discipline, conscientious behaviour, self-worth, caring, compassion, duty, empathy, generosity of spirit, integrity, responsibility, respect, dignity, courtesy, grace, joy, decency, innocence, and the celebration of life (did I miss any?). All of these qualities are dependent on the retention of self-respect. They are not characteristics that are developed. We cannot be educated into them. They are inherent but incapacitated by inadvertently clinging to a mournful aspect of our animal heritage.

Final word

I was just thinking of one of the phrases from the Flower Power movement, "Make love, not war." Were they like me, just having tremendous difficulty breaking through and grasping the elusive detail well enough to explain? Did they just miss the self-aware detail that would have read, "Make love, not lust"?

The initial belief that there was something wrong, that life should not consist of brutal pain, misery, and dystopia has been there throughout my life. It was only the thundering awareness of the source of our ills that finally threw me back on my heels with full realization. The simplicity of its resolution, even more so.

It has been an exasperatingly difficult effort to coherently decipher, face, and reveal the most inhibiting, insidious, and deeply embedded paradigms that have led mankind astray and, then, articulate those results. I can sympathize with the originator(s) of Pandora's Box. In my previous book, *Sentience,* my flailing first attempts are evident, even after twenty revisions. Thanks to those few that could read between the lines. It gave me heart to carry on. The previous book requires an intuitive sense, other than the chapter on how a man can learn to keep it up and insights regarding making love. That chapter is crystal clear, though further clarity is sure to come as we finally, enthusiastically explore the subject matter.

Every man definitely should read *Sentience.* Women should also read it to understand what a man needs to do, what men have endured, help guide and encourage a man's success, gain further insights into the situation, and consider their own ways in which to bolster the situation. I have tried to avoid too many insubstantial insights regarding the woman's perspective. I would only be guessing.

There is no doubt more will be learned on the subject of good sex as many begin to explore the subject openly but, the book should allow any man to physically love a woman thoroughly. The book also contains further notes on our deluded state and further evidence regarding the situation.

The best I can come up with as a description of the genre of this rather unusual effort is speculative non-fiction. There is little speculation left. Mankind can be much more than a beast.

Three generations

Our existence will never be a sinecure. This universe holds no promises. But, once the angst that drives men is overcome, we can easily abandon the millennia of nonsense that we have developed. It is the only way we gain our sanity. The polarization of mankind begins with the polarization of men and women and, thus, the misogyny and sexism that so defines every aspect of our current conditions and sentient failure.

Within one hundred years of the momentum of a sentient perspective beginning to take hold, we will look back on the insanity of our past with horror. Human versus monkey will be seen in stark, obvious contrast.

It seems it will take at least three generations to achieve some semblance of self-aware sanity. The first generation will still have been conditioned from birth into delusion. They will find some relief as they overcome the lack and begin to change the landscape of conditioning that their children absorb, but their own conditioning should linger to some extent. The following generation will enter into puberty with less pre-programmed conditioning to wreak havoc on their outlook, as father-son conversations begin to have meaning. The third generation should be able to begin dismantling the distortions to our existence in earnest.

Everything you see and do, your perspective, is influenced by the conditioning absorbed since your time of birth. So far, it has been a sad charade in which we have all participated. It has continued the illusion that dystopia should be expected and that we must slog our way out of the muck.

Uninhibited caring for another is a transcendent change that overcomes the self-centric perspective of the animal to reveal a comprehensive sentient perspective. Love is the natural, fulfilling, and sentiently-intrinsic state that results.

The idea that we must educate our way out of dystopia always bothered me. It also meant that what little sense we have could be knocked back to the stone age if we lost our formal education. That is not true of sentient sex. It is easily passed on from father to son, thus stabilizing self-aware sentience against any conditions in ways that a formal education never could. This is the only concept that needs to become commonly understood.

The pebble

You may notice that there is scant evidence of criticism of women in these books. It's not that there aren't lots of flaws in the way in which women go about life and sex. It is just that it all stems from men not admitting that they so disastrously bad at sex.

This is why the woman's voice has been suppressed in every aspect. Their gentle, unassuming sentient perspective provides for their relative silent consideration. They still maintain some ability to think. The fear has always been that women, as they are beginning to do, may actually speak out about the inconsistencies of our existence.

The situation becomes more confused and tentative as we flounder. Only men can resolve the situation before it becomes any more of an issue of confrontation and despair.

Deep in their despairing hearts, men, especially, have known what is missing all along. It is just that they accept excuses in desperation, clouding the issue. Women have always been an easy mark. It was easier to excuse poor performance and accept the already accomplished subjugation of women. The intimidating hurdle of successful sex seemed too much and was easily set aside. No real insights were ever garnered. They can't even explore because they cannot admit the lack openly.

The situation that women endure today is pitiful. The available options are to either avoid men avidly, tolerate men's aberrant behaviour, fight it to no avail, or become subservient and join them in the delusion. It must feel like drowning as men blindly bluster on. The possibility of finding a man that fulfills the manly task is remote and never relieves the possibility of other men's offensive treatment. The most farcical situation in this land of insanity is accepting a man as a 'protector' from other men.

The confusion concerning our situation has certainly infected women. They accepted men's poor performance as just the way it is for very good reasons. How could they possibly find the insight to improve men's performance enough to count when men couldn't? What would have been the point of bringing it up?

Through it all, though, the woman's sentience has never been compromised directly to the extent that men have endured. Women need not excuse their own failure, only the lack of their own satisfaction. Some few women have been our guiding light.

Our conditioning created a self-fulfilling prophecy. It is certain that no man desires to be poor at sex. We were just so convinced that it could never change, that humanity never really took the prospect seriously. We never really studied the problem. No man will purposely avoid learning to make love once they accept that it is possible. Fulfilled love-making is the ultimate residence for hope. We will expand on those insights ad infinitum.

The longer I think on it, making love is like nature's last hurdle to achieve full self-awareness. It begins the avalanche that unleashes our fully sentient qualities. It is a required hurdle for a race to achieve a sentient perspective, thus assuring our worthiness of the crown of sentience. Nature gifted us with the potential only. We have so far avoided the mirror of self-awareness and, thus, the achievement of loving sex.

Achieving a fully sentient perspective is up to us. Self-awareness only becomes a valuable gift once we overcome the conditions that impede its fulfillment. What makes our past most appalling is that the obstacle itself is not that difficult to overcome. The awe I feel for nature's subtle plan is indescribable.

Consider a situation in which increasingly destructive violence, fear, and confusion towards one's own race are the primary motivators of a race of semi-aware, disturbed beings. Now, look around. It is the situation we have inadvertently endured all along.

Details, details

I didn't want to get into distractions in the flow of the book but there is one topic that keeps coming to mind. Throughout this book, I note that mankind only needs protection from *itself*.

That is not an entirely accurate. More exactly, but distracting from the main topic, is to say that mankind only needs protection from itself *so far*. The reasons this fine distinction continues to gnaw at me are as follows.

As we explore further, we may come across other species with similar, or more, advanced capabilities. If an alien race has a similar disturbing past, which seems more than likely, is it possible that they have not set aside their rabid tendencies? Are we at risk of facing a race that is still aberrant and irrationally violent? While it seems unlikely, it is a distinct possibility that must be considered. Would gaining our sentience hobble us?

As I have noted over and over again, a species that does not acquire its sanity seems most likely to destroy or cripple itself. So, any race more advanced than ourselves should never be a threat. If they have achieved advancement well beyond us, I wholeheartedly believe they will have settled any disturbance within themselves. The internal conflict destroys. But, that still remains to be proven.

More to the point, I just cannot believe that a rabid race of remotely similar capabilities could possibly overcome a race that has learned to accept its sentience fully. I have been very careful never to suggest that we will become lotus-eaters, satisfied to do nothing. That is closer to our current bewildered state than one that is fulfilled. We will be more successful and industrious in the absence of dystopia. The point will never be to allow some fool to bash one over the head, whether human or otherwise. We protect ourselves and our race most thoroughly, most competently by accepting our sentience fully. A fully sentient race has less to fear, even if some rabid, advanced beings exist.

Well, I won't go further. The real situation concerning all of the future think subjects, such as AI and aliens, could fill a library. Just to say that, in all cases, an emotionally balanced, reasoning race will have a radically different view from the paranoid tomfoolery we consume so easily. Such a race has the best chance of survival.

Tolerance

Most people *seem* to tolerate this existence very well. Considering the misery that is sensed in most people, it is nothing more than endurance of an intolerable situation. We do our best to pretty it up but, to some extent, it is misery for all. Many dream of something better and, thus, adopt some escapism or alternative petty obsessions. Others just accept the dystopia, immersing themselves in its pain in a different form of escapism. Others try to buy their way out, which is just another form of delusion. Blind, indulgent, or unrepentant, it's all the same. It is delusion.

The banter and smiles are in spite of the pain of a semi-sentient race's cruel and devious existentialism. Life becomes numbness and learned endurance rather than celebration. It is a desperate attempt at compromise with a bewildering situation. A situation that becomes more dangerous every day.

The accepted definition of sanity, though it is never stated as such, is toleration for the insanity of our existence. We are considered sane when we blithely endure the insanity and misery usually for one's own benefit above all else.

All because men couldn't keep it up. It's no grand conspiracy. We are all faced with the quandary and arrive at some compromise with the situation that has never included staring directly into the face of the lack originating in the non-sentient animal. I certainly believe there must be other men that have completely overcome the bane. They are just too few to make a difference and none ever peered beyond their own situation to comprehend the full ramifications due to the current programmed selfish context.

Sentience is not the root cause of our troubles. It is just the simplest target for our mindless ire in avoidance of the real issue. Intellect and self-awareness are the reasons we recognize that animal sex is incomplete. That is not a bad thing. The accompanying intellect allows us to overcome the lack.

Some with whom I have interacted like to say that we are not screwed up. It is just the curse of sentience, thus, grin and bear it (the current definition of sanity) to one's own advantage. This, initially, threw me back on my heels so hard that it caused bruises. They numb themselves to the seething state and fully embrace the selfish brute.

Do the destitute and poverty-stricken of mankind not suggest that something is deeply wrong in the heart and soul of mankind? We are supposed to accept that mankind is meant for misery? Our brilliant minds are so stupid that we cannot overcome these lacks and to hell with the downtrodden?

The pervasive misogyny and domestic violence (never fully acknowledged! or explained!) are somehow to be expected? All of the perversions of human life, especially concerning sex, are natural? So, to hell with women, as well? The Dorian Grays are much more common than anyone imagines. What could possibly cause us to understate these ongoing, devastating conditions?

The selfish perspective of the animal dominates. An undercurrent of instability propels us. We are our own blindspot. We write off bizarre behaviour as something that must be treated rather than admit to mankind's insane situation and its cause. Our instability is never considered symptomatic of a derangement that grips mankind. We use pontificating TLA's to describe the inability to endure our insanity and write it off.

The way in which we live makes sense to you? Proclaim suicide a crime and stuff surviving perpetrators full of stupor-inducing medication or fit them for a straight-jacket because they recognize, and poorly endure, our lunacy and misery? We talk them off the ledge convincing them that everything is really alright rather than address the underlying reasons they desire a way out.

The answer is not hiding our heads in the sand nor proclaiming humanity despicable. The answer is not insubstantially suggesting that we are getting better or ending one's life. The answer lies not in fending only for oneself. The answer is not escape into fantasy. We have avoided an inspection of mankind for far too long. The distractions we bring to the situation are appalling.

We convince ourselves that enduring the misery is the answer. In our confusion and delusion, tolerance of misery and brutality equates with sanity. The many that bend until they break due to mankind's bestial dystopia are flawed. Right.

The point is that we have never taken a close look at mankind itself yet. Our gaze always veers away because that is where the secret of our (unnecessary) failure lies. That must now change and we must scrutinize mankind closely as we shed the source of our most insidious delusions, and obsessions.

Our cyclical existence that is repeated throughout history, always leading to war, while everyone stands around feeling helpless is to be expected? The wars, insane righteousness, justifications, manipulation, pompous meddling in everyone else's affairs, abuses and corruption of the systems and structures of mankind are symptomatic signs that something is seriously wrong.

We are not that dumb, though we are that blinded! The revolutions invariably just indulge the pent-up fury, frustration, and aggravation with no other lasting result.

Those with some modicum of empathy tolerate the increasingly selfish behaviour and greed until they finally break, curl up in a ball or explode. Make no mistake, it is getting worse, not better, as our intelligence and ability to manipulate the universe and each other progress. We must turn around, look in the mirror, and face the real reason for our insanity. So far, there have been two choices, misery or a selfish cloak of insensitivity.

The most insensitive and self-centered decide that nothing is wrong, throw the downtrodden a bone, and go on to wreak havoc.

Sometimes, now that I've shed a good deal of the conditioning, I look around in shock. What is the matter with us? It's like humanity wants to punish itself for being human. The belief that we are cursed is accepted by an animal in pain. We hate ourselves so thoroughly that we desperately seek reasons to hate and despise others by highlighting their slightest differences.

From Voltaire to Lennon to Dylan (either) to Shakespeare to Elliot to Heinlein to Clarke and Freud, when it comes to *humanity itself*, the supposedly great authors of our past have never attempted to see past the pain. They only indulge it, never exploring that which should be and why it is missing. We have always accepted the rear view mirror, or what is right in front of our noses, or escape into imagined fantasy, when it comes to humanity itself. The authors are applauded for their insights into the depths of our depravity. It is time for a change. Exploiting, glorifying, and picking at the scabs on the wound that destroys our existence is the chore and pastime of a simpleton. It's time for the glorified desperation and misery of mankind to give way to deep thought on achieving the magnificent work of art that mankind should be. Magnificence is in us, if we can only see.

Anyone that has gotten this far has some wit about them and must be getting the message to some extent. So, let me put it in certain terms. The importance of mutually fulfilling sex is laid bare and it can be accomplished. The way we will finally interpret the situation is this. Any male that does not invoke the necessary insight and discipline to fulfill and care for a woman emotionally and sexually remains an animal.

Women have convinced themselves that something else disturbed men or accepted men's lack as insurmountable. They can no longer afford to do so. Good loving is not something to be weighed in the scales of a relationship for a woman. It is a precondition to humanity. At this point, maybe just finding a man willing to find some way to provide satisfaction, while continuing to explore how to provide eye to eye satisfaction, is enough.

It may take a few generations for mankind to fully engage the spark of sentience and become whole. It all starts with the effort of men to become lovers rather than just taking their own selfish pleasure. It is an effort requiring only the slightest amount of the discipline, wit, and knowledge of a fully self-aware being.

It is crucial to acknowledge this dilemma of ours for a number of reasons. Firstly, we can overcome anything we set our minds to, if we don't blind ourselves, if we make a concerted effort to overcome. We are so accepting of our dismal state that it is appalling. We must fully overcome this failure eye to eye in a sentient manner without bestial adaptations. In other words, it has to be something human, not concocted in a lab or factory. It has to support the self-respect of the individuals involved. We become fully human once we learn to make love eye to eye.

Secondly, acknowledging that the woman's sexual satisfaction is part of the human equation changes the perspective. We leave the beast behind, once we admit that fact.

Thirdly, it is the *only* way in which to achieve equality. It is the only way to finally gain our humanity. It is providing the woman's satisfaction in a loving fashion that changes everything. The ability to love a woman eye to eye is the most fulfilling way that can be achieved. It is worth every effort to get there.

There are two unanswered questions over all of the long millennia that have crippled our existence. The one concerning the resolution that we have avoided, is answered in *Sentience.* The answer to the other critical question is that we endure the delusion that we are no better than rutting animals because we avoided the first question. Avoiding both questions obfuscated self-awareness and created our miserable conditions.

There is a third question. What is different about our sentience? The first full glimmer of heightened self-awareness is found in primates, but the complete resolution can only be attained by a fully self-aware race. Apes just began to get a clue.

I really wish this were as simple to explain and understand as "don't bash your neighbor over the head". Unfortunately, that is not the case. It will take some slight amount of effort for us to shed our bestial stupor. We have been battered by nonsense and violence at every point in our daily lives. It is no small task to finally become fully sentient. We can only begin by freeing our sentient perceptions from their delusions to achieve a sentient perspective.

Self-aware sentience and making love are good!

This has been the story of mankind up until this point in time. You get to choose what happens next. As fully self-aware beings, something more is required of us. How about we just leave the chaos and the muck behind? We can be free. Make it so. What we can finally achieve is beyond my comprehension.

My poetry and Gypsy Empress were the keys with which I began to unlock the secrets of Sentient Love. I hope this book does the same for you.

w

whickwithy@gmail.com
https://sentienceww.blogspot.com/

Love-making is an incredibly intuitive term, the full details of which I will leave for you to explore. That single word (or combinatorial word?) is so exact and precise in meaning, yet, just like the word love, we have diminished and ignored its true meaning and significance.

Love is completely incapacitated by the lack that we endure. By the way, an interesting exercise is to go through this book and, in every case, replace the word sentient with the word loving and the word sentience with love.

To emphasize the most important goal and concept that will be released from its fetters as we gain a sentient perspective, to be consistent and purposeful, the very final word of this missive must be love.